Mary Anne Hearn

Lays and Lyrics of the Blessed Life

Consisting of light from the cross, and other poems

Mary Anne Hearn

Lays and Lyrics of the Blessed Life
Consisting of light from the cross, and other poems

ISBN/EAN: 9783744796361

Printed in Europe, USA, Canada, Australia, Japan

Cover: Foto ©Thomas Meinert / pixelio.de

More available books at **www.hansebooks.com**

LAYS AND LYRICS:

OF

THE BLESSED LIFE,

CONSISTING OF

LIGHT FROM THE CROSS,

AND

Other Poems.

BY

MARIANNE FARNINGHAM.

"Is it not strange the darkest hour
That ever dawned on sinful earth
Should touch the heart with softer power
For comfort than an angel's mirth?
That to the Cross the mourner's eye should turn,
Sooner than wher the stars of Christmas burn?"

J. KEBLE.

NINTH EDITION.

London:

JAMES CLARKE & CO., 13, FLEET STREET.

1872.

AUTHOR'S PREFACE TO FIRST EDITION.

WITH a fervent "God-speed" this lowly warbler of the valley spreads wing, singing loving lays, though its songs may not excel in strength, nor its plumage possess beauty enough to win praise from impartial ears and eyes.

But if you, dear Reader, favour it so highly as to allow it to become a welcome guest in your happy home,—if in the twilight, or by the glowing fire, surrounded by loving ones, amid mirth and joy, or alone with the yearnings of your own spirit, it bring to you tender thoughts, as from a sister who presses the same steep hill-side as yourself, with the same aims, and hopes, and fears; and journeying, as she trusts you are also, to our "Father's house,"—if it but make "the Blessed Life" more alluring to one undecided, or more pleasant and satisfying, even amid its difficulties, to one disciple of Jesus—then surely a portion of time redeemed from other mental engagements will not have been thus occupied in vain; and the writer will rejoice greatly, feeling amply rewarded for all the toils of her congenial task.

She knows how faltering and imperfect are her best efforts,— that her experience must of necessity fall far short of that of some who may peruse these pages, and who have lived many years amid the scenes and lessons she only *begins* to understand; yet she ventures this public expression of her feelings in the hope that others may sympathize with them.

MARIANNE FARNINGHAM.

December, 1861.

PUBLISHER'S PREFACE TO FIFTH EDITION.

Four large editions of this book have been sold within the space of four years; and now that a fifth edition is demanded, the Publisher feels constrained to take advantage of the opportunity afforded to unite with the gifted Author in warm acknowledgments to the Christian public for the generous welcome that has thus been given to the work. Its success has far exceeded the most sanguine anticipations; though certainly no person familiar with its contents will hesitate to admit that even yet the circulation of the volume has greatly fallen short of its manifest merits, whether regarded in its poetical or its religious aspects. There is much consolation in the assurance that a spiritual blessing has gone with the book in various directions. Since its first issue, a multitude of communications have been received expressive of the delight and benefit imparted by the perusal of the poems. They have often ministered pleasure to the social and family circle, and have carried the sunshine of hope into the abodes of many lonely and afflicted ones, causing them to think lightly of present sufferings in anticipation of the "pleasures for evermore."

In the confident conviction that thousands of other homes will be similarly cheered and blessed by these Lays and Lyrics, this new and revised edition is sent forth, commended to all whose hearts yearn after the beautiful and the true, and who "hold and are held" by that Cross whose influence alone enables mankind to use this world as not abusing it, and to look forward without dismay to the world that is to come.

London, November, 1866.

CONTENTS.

CONTENTS.

LAYS AND LYRICS,

ETC.

Light from the Cross.

O FOR an angel's power of mind and thought!
  The earth-bound soul can only weakly seem
To tell of that with such deep meaning fraught,
  That angels stand astonished at the theme.
Light from the Cross!—O, may it gild my page,
  Irradiate my mind, and nerve my hand
To write of things which still from age to age
  Will form the songs they sing in spirit land.

How deep the darkness that, with gloomy wings,
  Sat brooding o'er the world ere this light shone,
Throwing more mystery o'er hidden things,
  Shrouding the soul that sat and sighed alone!
Glory to God! for now, athwart the skies,
  Light from the Cross of Calvary has come,
To shed its blessed beams upon our eyes,
  And thus illuminate the pathway home.

Softly its rays shone on the history
  Of man's first sin against his holy God,
Unfolding on the scene the mystery
  Of his redemption through a Saviour's blood,
Lighting the fearful sentences of death
  On the closed gates of long-lost Paradise,
And upward urging the aspiring breath
  To a far better Eden in the skies.

Light from the Cross upon God's broken law!
  The trembling soul shrank from its Maker's look,
Until, with heavenly-lighted eyes, it saw
  Hope for the sinner in the Holy Book.
Mount Sinai's top was covered with the cloud
  Of the Eternal's anger, till on high,
"Look unto Calvary!" was proclaimed aloud,
  And sunbeams spread o'er all the brightening sky.

And we, who break it still, who work and strive
  But to increase our own unrighteousness,
When fainting 'neath our burden, may revive,
  As closer to that lighted Cross we press:
For "Christ fulfilled the law," and we may cling
  To that fulfilment as our perfect good;
Beneath His holiness our sins may fling,
  And see our natures pardoned and renewed.

Light from the Cross irradiates the time
  Of types and shadows, with their misty air;
Throws over it a glory all sublime,
  That ere it shone was never witnessed there:
The olden service, and the sacrifice
  Of bulls and goats, and offerings for sin,
Were but the shadows of that wondrous price
  Paid on the Cross our rebel souls to win.

The lamb, without a blemish, that was laid
  On Israel's sacred altar, and the fire
That kindled when their offerings were made,
  And bore to heaven their penitent desire,
Were only simple types of Him who came
  To be the "Lamb of God," and take away
The world's dark heritage of sin and shame—
  Our sacrifice, whose power can ne'er decay.

And so when we have sinned, and wildly weep,
  Not to these outward rites our spirits turn;
When God's just wrath shall round about us sweep,
  Our worn hearts for a purer offering yearn.
The lamp of Calvary will guide us where
  He lives—the spotless Lamb who once was slain;
His blood is sprinkled on us in our prayer,
  And we are washed and pure from every stain.

Light from the Cross has shone on prophecy,
  That dark, uncertain page of baffling power;
And man may read it now with kindling eye,
  And list the oracles all dumb before.
Strange beauty gilds the sacred words inspired,
  Lessons Divine are radiant with its beams;
Man sees what ancient prophets long desired,
  And sings of Calvary by way-side streams.

How sweet Isaiah's words of eloquence,
  And Jeremiah's pathos to us, now
That light has elevated human sense,
  And glory touched the aching, dust-soiled brow!
Christ came to preach good tidings to the meek,
  To loose the captives, broken hearts to bind,
To comfort Zion's mourners, and to seek
  The lost and wretched whom none else could find.

Ah! could the throngs whom thus the prophets taught,
　Who heard and marvelled, but believed them not,
Within the Gospel's radiance have been brought,
　They had not then the wondrous words forgot:
The holy cities where our fathers praised,
　And fields and valleys, would all vocal be,
And from Judæa's mountain-tops be raised
　One long glad hymn of Christian melody.

Light from the Cross upon the promises!
　How sweet their life-words to the sickened soul!
Healing, and solace, and support in these
　Are found, grief's surging billows to control:
They who have sat beneath the Cross may take
　And bind them ever to the grateful heart,
Their own blest heritage for Jesus' sake,
　To calm the terror and allay the smart.

There was a weary, way-worn, wandering man,
　Who groped amid the darkness of the earth,
Who read with eye-sight dim the Gospel plan,
　Nor understood its beauty or its worth;
But when he knelt before the holy Cross,
　And saw that weary ones might sweetly rest,
How did he call all other treasures loss,
　And clasp the promise to his throbbing breast!

Light from the Cross upon the history
　Of falling nations and a changing world,
Explaining brightly the deep mystery—
　Some peoples raised, and some to ruin hurled.
Where'er this light has dawned, the hand of God
　Is seen disposing the intricacies,
Bringing a brighter period with His nod,
　When all shall know the Saviour—all be his.

And now it melts the Greenland heart of ice,
    Softens the fierce will of the African,
Throws beauty round the Indian's wild device,
    And crowns with heavenly flowers the Mexican.
And war and pestilence, where'er they go,
    But pioneer the blessed time of peace,
When every tribe shall our Jehovah know,
    And powers destructive in His mild reign cease.

Light from the Cross upon that spotless Life
    That trod, in human flesh, this vale of tears,
Turning to harmony the din of strife,
    Staying with love earth's agony and fears!
A stranger 'midst His own, He suffered here,
    Till, on the Cross uplifted, there was given
Conviction to His murderers; while fear
    Seized those who crucified the King of Heaven!

Light on the miracles the Saviour wrought,
    Light on the healing touch of that kind hand,
On all the blessings, with such mercy fraught,
    He scattered broadcast on the thirsty land!
The wondering crowd were fain to own that He
    Must be Messiah—such His matchless power—
Who made the lame to walk, the blind to see,
    And raised the dead from its unlighted hour.

He fed the weary, hungry multitude;—
    Light from the Cross proves Him the living bread:
Among His people, poor, despised, He stood;—
    Light from the Cross proves Him their glorious head:
He healed the sick as they around Him pressed;—
    This light shows Him the healer of our souls:
He soothed the raging tempest-waves to rest;—
    And He our passion and our sin controls.

Light from the Cross falls on our mission here,
  Lights up the path of duty for our feet,
Turns to sublimity this lower sphere,
  And makes our daily labour light and sweet.
It quickens to activity the nerve
  That sluggish lies in hearts too faint and cold,
The " Well done, faithful servant," to deserve,
  In that blest city where the streets are gold.

The missionary sees it, and is strong
  To labour on, though death is all around;
The pastor hails it, and can raise a song,
  Though cares and sorrows in his lot abound;
It falls upon the teacher's darkened room,
  And more than mortal strength at once is given;
It warms and cheers the suffering martyr's gloom,
  And lights his spirit with a ray of heaven.

Light from the Cross upon the miseries
  That crowd around the way-worn pilgrim here,
Hope for the wretched in his poverties,
  Joy for the sufferer in his lowest sphere!
O! 'twere enough to make the angels weep,
  To watch the outcasts in their great distress,
Deep shadows brooding o'er them as they sleep;
  But even here this light has made it less.

Hundreds of ragged little ones, who bear
  Faintly indeed the stamp of childhood's joy,
Were watching willingly each lurking snare,
  Waiting to find from Satan some employ:
But there were Christian hearts and active feet,
  Which trod the darkened haunts of wretchedness,
And brought them from their places of retreat,
  Intent, like Jesus Christ, to aid and bless.

And now, throughout our happy Christian land,
  What groups of sweet young faces may be seen,
Singing with joy of Jesus as they stand,
  With bright intelligence of eye and mien;
Learning deep lessons how to live and die,
  To play their parts as in God's holy sight;
While prayers are breathed that they beyond the sky
  May praise Him ever for this blessed light!

Light from the Cross upon the cottagers
  That toil from morn till night for daily bread!
A lot of hunger is too often theirs,
  Of sleepless tossing on their rough, hard bed;
But light has power to reach their humble home,
  Power the intensest darkness to dispel,
To lead to Calvary all those who roam,
  And make them own at last, God doeth well!

Through the dark alleys, with a silent prayer,
  Aurelia wends her dim, intricate way :
Daughter of Luxury! what doth she there?
  See, many a rough voice urges her to stay!
She brings them light their darksome way to cheer,
  She tells them softly of the Saviour's love—
How 'twas the poor He loved and sought while here,
  And that He pities them, though now above.

She leaves the Bible there, and so each night
  The poor man sits upon his wooden chair,
While shines around his home the Gospel light,
  And the rude walls are vocal with his prayer.
O! blessings on that true, warm woman's heart,
  That in her love and trust did what she could;
And praise to Him who did His light impart,
  And fill her spirit with such gratitude!

B

Light from the Cross sometimes, with holy beam.
　Has fallen upon the drunkard's sodden mind,
Awaking him from his delirious dream,
　His true position in the world to find;
And the wine-cup is quickly dashed aside,
　For higher impulses attend him now;
He is a man again with manly pride,
　And the dark blot is fading from his brow.

There was a man in whose black, kindling eye
　The fever-fires of passion wildly burned;
His was the harsh rebuke, the rude reply,
　The haughty spirit that his fellows spurned:
But once, when the sweet Sabbath bell was rung,
　He lingered near the Cross a little while;
And now the words of love are on his tongue,
　The lion is a lamb, with patient smile.

Another, too, there was, who lightly spoke
　The holy name of the Almighty God,
Who in the minds of others oft awoke
　A wish to tread the sinful paths he trod.
But a strong hand was on him, and he knelt
　Beside the Cross, until its brilliant light
Fell on his spirit, and the scoffer felt
　Humbled and penitent in Jesus' sight.

Thrice-blessed, holy light! where'er it shines
　Its sacred influence at once is known;
It moulds the hardest heart, until it twines
　In lowly, reverent love around the throne.
So noiseless, yet so infinite its sway,
　It spreads like lucent sunbeams o'er the earth;
And joyfully the hearts of men obey,
　And waken to a more exalted birth.

All that is good, or great, or high, or pure,
    Springs from that one great fountain at the Cross;
That is the only good that will endure
    When other gains are proved but constant loss!
That nerves the painter's hand and guides his dreams;
    The poet and the sculptor own its power:
God is the source of art, and Calvary's beams
    Give it a glory never seen before.

For science flourishes amid its light,
    And literature attains a higher tone,
And courtesy, and kindness, with delight,
    Will ever make the Christian land their own.
Our country's greatness from this light proceeds;
    The Gospel makes it noble, good, and free,
And yet within its sod are but the seeds;—
    What will the great and glorious harvest be?

I hear the indistinct slow Future's tramp,
    Marching along the beaten way of Time;
In its broad hands it bears the Gospel lamp,
    And on its lofty brow God's seal sublime!
What shall the destiny of nations be—
    What the grand future of this rising world,—
When Jesus' Gospel shall have set them free,
    And He the banner of His Cross unfurled?

Ah! who can paint that glorious time of good,
    When the dark corners of the earth shall come
And join their hearts and hands in brotherhood,
    All pilgrims to the universal home?
When war shall never raise its clanging noise,
    Nor hands be lifted but to clasp and bless;
Good-will and peace prevail—earth's greatest joys—
    And warm kind hearts of brethren, in distress?

Where, then, shall ignorance be ? O, man may seek,
But never find it, in that happy hour:
And vice will triumph not above the weak ;
It shall be conquered by a higher power :
And superstition, with its wearing rust,
And enmity, with its sly, creeping tread,
Will then give room to perfect love and trust,
Calling down blessings on each other's head.

Light from the Cross shall be the world's great weal;
All moral benefits from thence have sprung;
And its unfolding changes shall reveal
How God His blessings round the Cross has flung.
The Saviour teaches morals to mankind;
The lofty character proceeds from Him ;
And he who copies Jesus in his mind
Will have an excellence years cannot dim.

And in the good time coming man will be
A nobler creature, because more like God,
For the rich light of Christianity
Shall be diffused as sunshine all abroad.
And this shall be the secret of the change :—
The great predictions shall have been fulfilled;
Man kneels before his Maker, glad t' exchange
His best performances for Christ's blood spilled.

And nations, in one concert grand and deep,
Will learn calm lessons at the Holiest's feet ;
Their hearts in Calvary's streams will seek to steep,
And bring to heaven the praises that are meet.
Here only perfect holiness is found :
Before the Cross man ceases thus to strive,
Lies in abasement on the blood-washed ground,
Grateful his all from Jesus to derive.

Light from the Cross upon the followers
   Of Christ, the Spotless One! Sometimes 'tis dim;
While earth-clouds float above these lives of theirs
   They are not perfect followers of Him.
Not conquered quite as yet is Satan's power:
   Faith, Hope, and Charity are not quite strong;
They falter sometimes in the trying hour,
   And grieve the God to whom they all belong.

But, with the full refulgence of that light,
   Full holiness will deck the Christian's brow;
He will be beautiful in Jesus' sight,
   If in His righteousness alone he bow.
And deeper are the lessons Christ will teach,
   The longer they remain in His blest school,
And higher the attainments they will reach,
   While He who is all tenderness shall rule.

The perfect Christian is the perfect man;
   Morality and excellence must be
With those who know and feel the Gospel plan:
   Whom God has honoured, Jesus has set free.
All gentleness, and purity, and love,
   Call this their birth-place, where the streams that flow
Are preparations for that state above
   Which shall no sin or darkness ever know!

A child is playing 'mid the bright, gay flowers,
   A maiden dreams in the sweet twilight dim,
A youth is singing through the sunny hours,
   And manhood's voice swells high the holy hymn.
Why are they all so happy? 'Tis that they
   Have gathered silently around the Cross,
And, therefore, joys that cannot fade away
   Are theirs, e'en in this world of grief and loss.

Light from the Cross! How bright the mercy-seat
  Is to the timid soul approaching now!
How passing dear the place at Jesus' feet,
  Where she can look to Calvary and bow;
Where hopes all heaven-born fill the expanding mind,
  And love eternal satisfies the heart;
Where its weak tendrils fondly are entwined
  Around the Highest, never more to part!

So when our yearning spirits cry for peace,
  And we are left with all our griefs alone,
Within that sacred place the storm will cease,
  And we gain access to the blood-washed throne.
No sword of vengeance drives the soul away,
  But Jesus welcomes with His beaming smile,
When in our wretchedness we turn to pray,
  And bask in that blest sunlight for a while.

And when with undimmed power that light shall shine,
  Those who are bound in Christian unity
Shall love as brethren in those rays divine,
  Shall hope and suffer all in charity,
Shall quell the flashing glance, the selfish thought,
  And cultivate the loving word and deed,
In characters with such high goodness fraught
  That all men shall confess them Christ's indeed.

And then our grand cathedrals will not be
  Closed to God's servants of another name;
Nor those who love each other disagree,
  Their hopes, their fears, their interests the same.
The party spirit will not then distress
  Those who kneel down at the same throne of grace;
But lips that coldly sneered will warmly bless,
  All longing eagerly for Jesus' face.

O happy period! Blessed, holy light!
Would that our eyes might see, our ears might hear,
Its kindling rays dispel the gloomy night;
Would that "the good time coming" might be near!
Our eyes are straining for it evermore;
Our hearts have ceased not for its dawn to pray!
O that the hours of darkness were but o'er!
O that the reign of light would not delay!

Light from the Cross dawns on affliction's night;
Dreams—angel-dreams float oft amid the pain,
Making the rod that rests upon us light,
Helping the spirit rise and trust again:
For in God's characters of love we read
What tender, useful offices are theirs,
How trials are God's children's greatest need,
How "loving-kindness" sends their deepest cares.

Yon lonely sufferer, whose friends have passed
On long before her to the Great Unseen,
Is not unhappy, though she is the last
Of a large joyous circle that has been;
For there is glory round about her bed,
And she can see, e'en with her aged eyes,
The light of Calvary above her head,
Wooing her gently to her native skies.

Light from the Cross illumines scenes of joy,
Gives to our pleasure all its richest glow,
Suggests the holy themes our thoughts employ,
Lends rays of heaven to these fleet hours below;
Guides ever higher to that land of love,
Where crystal waters and green pastures be;
And fills the heart that yearns for things above
With quiet hopes of immortality.

Light from the Cross upon the vale of death:
No longer is it heralded by gloom;
For when its icy hand has stayed the breath,
Light from the Cross will radiate on the tomb;
And cheerfully toward that home serene
The trusting soul will speed upon its way,
Till, basking in God's light—no veil between—
Darkness and doubt and death will flee away.

So dies the Christian! Shadows only come
Across the valley which he needs must tread;
There is no terror frighting him from home;
He will be there when others say " He's dead!"
He does not fear the narrow resting-place,
'Tis but the lighted threshold of his heaven;
Angels are round him with the torch of grace—
Soon the full blaze of glory will be given.

Light from the Cross will not grow dim above;
The shining robe, the golden harp, will be
But tokens of the Saviour's deathless love,
Who hung on Calvary to set us free.
And through eternity the swelling song
Will celebrate the wonders of that light
That beamed our chequered earthly path along,
And brought us safely where there's no more night.

Praise for the blessed light of Calvary!
O! when *our* tongues are loosed, a noble hymn
Shall praise Him for the glory constantly,
That e'en these earth-damps cannot shade or dim.
Till then, whate'er of trial's power may come,
Let us ne'er leave this blessed, holy place;—
Beneath the Cross of Christ shall be our home,
Till we behold the Saviour face to face.

The Future.

" He shall choose our inheritance for us."—Psalm xlvii. 4.

THE lofty elms were waving to and fro,
And making solemn music. The brown leaves
Fell softly on the greensward. The pale stars
Looked on the sleeping earth, and smiled. The hush
Was deep and all unbroken, save the fall
Of a light footstep. For, with measured tread,
Beneath the spreading branches, one there walked
In whose strong frame, and flashing eye, and brow
High and unwrinkled, were the buoyancy
And strength of youth. He stood with halting feet
On manhood's threshold. He had just awoke
To see life as it is; with purposes,
And impulses, to make it something great
And worthy of its Donor. And he sought
To make his future course, and chose and dreamed
Of paths that he would like to tread; and yet,
Round all there gathered something like a mist
And dark uncertainty: there seemed to be
A doubt, and dread, and danger with the joy,
Whichever way he looked. And then he thought
Of One who in His mighty hand holds all
The destiny of nations, yet loves well
To be the Guide of youth. The young man bared
His head, and, glancing up to the high heavens,
Said, "Father, choose for me!"

Years passed away.
The strong athletic frame was called to bend

Beneath the weight of labour. And the scroll
Of his life's duties opened gradually.
He had a mission here. For him fond ties
Of close affection were not made. He saw
Families gather round his friends, and heard
Sweet epithets of tender love; but they
Were not for him. He might have chosen them;
But He who knoweth what is best for us
Withheld them all, and gave him wealth. And so
He fed the hungry, clothed the shivering form,
And lived and laboured as God's servants should.
And he was very happy. Those whom he
Had blessed called blessings down on him. And peace,
That peace that passeth knowledge, filled his heart
And satisfied its yearnings. And at last,
When the call came to bring him home, he said,
" Goodness and mercy follow all my days,
And I shall dwell within the house of God
For ever."

       .   .   .   .   ●   ●

            There was yet another—one
On whose fair forehead was a wreath of thought
And earnest meditation.

                   Future years
Lay spread before her. What the rolling tide
Might toss upon the sands of life, and what
Her path might be, she could not tell; and as
She sat before her window, and looked out
On the dim earth, she wished it might be hers
To scan that hidden landscape. But it passed—
That wild, impatient wish. She raised her eye,
Bright with the light of youth and hope, toward **heaven.**
The deep, deep azure made her think of Him

Whose great white throne is there. His mighty love
Had made her childhood beautiful. And He,
She knew, would bless her now. And so she prayed,
" Choose Thou my lot for me."
There pressed around
Friends with warm, loving hearts, who laid sweet flowers
Along her sunny path. Bright smiles there were
To welcome her where'er she went. And ties,
Fond, close, and sweet, bound her young heart to home
And dear old England. But, at last, there came
One dearer than the rest, noble and good ;
And their two life-streams mingled, and were ONE.
They watched the unseen guiding hand, and soon
It led them from the old home-scenes, to where
The dark-browed chieftain waited for the joy
Of God's salvation. It would be wrong
To say she shed no tears of parting. But
She knew the way He chose for her would be
The path of safety and of happiness !
And so she went with him who had become
Her earthly all ; and soon she left the home
So many loves had lighted, and became
The inmate of a lowly cot, beneath
A scorching sun, far from the happy scenes
Of cloudless childhood. Was she happy there ?
Ah, yes! for all the ease and rest and joy
Of her old fatherland, she would not leave
The spot where God has sent her. Every day
Had brought its meed of happiness,—and closed
With songs as glad and grateful as went up
From the home circle in the far-off land.

.   .   .   .

Yes ! surely it is better far that He
Choose our inheritance. We may be led

Through paths we imaged not.   But peace and joy
Go always where He leads.   We need not fear
The shadows in the distance.   Let us place
Our hand within our Father's, and commit
Our way to Him.

The Convert.

THE Romanists had gathered in
   The chapel wide and high ;
And solemnly the organ's peal
   Went up, as to the sky :
The burning candles threw a glare
   On pictured saints around,
While all the congregation knelt
   In silence on the ground.

The white-robed priests were chanting words
   In dialect unknown,
And so the ignorant were forced
   To worship all alone ;
They listened to the music's swell,
   And gazed upon the cross ;
And " use is second nature," so
   They thought not on their loss.

But one, the fairest of them all,
   Who formed that gorgeous scene,
A pale and thoughtful-looking girl,
   Whose years were just eighteen ;
Her quiet brow was very sad,
   She had an anxious look ;
And every now and then she touched
   A little hidden book.

She knelt as all the others did,
  And to the altar turned,
And bent her head in lowliness,
  While clouds of incense burned;
Yet, when they rose and left the place,
  She said with bitterness—
"O, what a mockery it is
  To worship God like this!"

And when she gained her father's house
  Her silent room she sought,
And closed the door most carefully,
  As if for quiet thought;
And, having softly gone into
  A little secret nook,
She quickly from her pocket drew
  The wondrous little book.

For many days she had perused
  Its pages o'er and o'er;
And now she conned it carefully,
  As she had done before:
And, as she read, fresh beauty seemed
  To beam upon her sight,
And silently her heart-thought rose—
  "Thy Word it giveth light."

She saw that Christ, and He alone,
  Could peace and pardon give—
Could teach the fallen sinner how
  In light and joy to live:
She saw how those who loved His name
  Must choose the better part—
With earth and all its vain delights
  Should be prepared to part.

She felt that all the false, dark creeds
    That had deceived her youth
Must be forsaken by her now,
    For they were not the truth ;
That even parents, friends, and home
    Were not her " all in all,"
And might not keep her where she was,
    If Christ should onward call.

And, though 'twas very hard, she felt
    That they could all be given
For the assurance of His love
    And one sure hope of heaven.
But, though she read the sacred Word,
    She could not trust in Him ;
And all her views of that best Friend
    Were incomplete and dim.

So, many earnest hours she spent
    Upon her knees in prayer ;
And supplications deep and strong
    Rose on the midnight air ;
She had no earthly teacher, but
    Her cries went up to God,
And soon the Saviour's smile beamed forth
    Upon the path she trod.

But the profession of her faith
    Provoked her father's ire,
And frowning priests were ushered in
    To talk of flaming fire ;
Those, too, whom she had fondly loved
    Now passed her coldly by,
Or spoke such angry, bitter words,
    She almost wished to die.

Yet stedfast 'midst it all she stood,
 And by her pleading love
Won many proud, mistaken hearts
 To seek for peace above!
In that bright world before the throne,
 Calmly she resteth now;
The palm of victory in her hand,
 The crown upon her brow.

Ruth's Resolve.

FRESHLY the morning air, with scented breath,
Came o'er the mountain tops. The yellow corn
Was ripening for harvest, and the sun
Shone out in splendour, as if glad to chase
Famine away from Judah. Everything
Looked lovely to the exiled Naomi:
She saw it all, but at her aching heart
Was such accumulated sorrow, that
Her spirit sank within her, and she turned
From the fair scene to muse upon her woe.
Into the land of Moab she had come,
Leaning upon her husband. He was strong,
And princely in his manhood; and his eyes
Had bent upon her with such looks of love
As they kept journeying, that she scarcely felt
The weariness of travel. By their side,
In the exuberance of laughing youth,
Their two fair sons had walked. But where were they

Now that she was returning?   The dark grave
Shrouded her best-beloved and beautiful :
And, with an aching, empty heart, she rose
To recommence her journey.   But there was
Another trial to be borne.   She called
The youthful, weeping widows, whom she loved
With all a mother's tenderness, who shared
So deeply in their grief, and bade them go
Back to their childhood's home.   Yet for a while
She stayed to bless them.   They had been so kind
And tender to her sons, and to herself!
Fervently she besought the Lord to bless them,
And, with a voice choked in its utterance, prayed
That other husbands might bind up their hearts,
And give them rest.   And then "they lifted up
Their voices, and they wept."   They would not go,
And leave her in her solitude; but she,
With stedfast heart of pure unselfishness,
In firm low tones, and words unfaltering,
Bade them depart to their ancestral homes.
Orpah returned.   But Ruth, the gentle Ruth,
Clave to her yet more closely, and her arms
Tightened around Naomi, till the tears
Gathered within her eyes, and her white lips
Quivered with feeling as she said, " Go back
Unto thy people!"   But the youthful head
Sank on her breast again, and she replied—

" Entreat me not to leave thee!   I have lived
So long in happiness by thy dear side,
So much of loving tenderness received,
I would for ever near to thee abide,
My mother!   Cherish me within thy heart,
            And bid me not depart!

"Where'er thou goest, let thy daughter go,
And lodge where'er thou liest down to rest;
Thine is the only God I wish to know,
And thine the people that I love the best;
Where'er thou diest, I will pray to die,—
   Where thou art buried, lie!

"O! for the sake of those we both have loved,
For the sweet memories of the happy past,
Let me not in thy sorrow be removed,
Let me stay with thee even to the last;
I cannot bear alone this early woe—
   O! bid me not to go!

"He who so cheered me with his manly love,
Is smiling on me while I ask thee now:
O! thou who lov'dst him, bid me not remove,
But stay and chase the anguish from thy brow.
Bid me stand by thee in thy hours of pain:
   Permit me to remain."

Naomi pressed her to her heart, and spake
No other words. And they both journeyed on
Unto the land of Judah. Ruth saw not
What there awaited her: but yet she felt
The joy of those who do a noble deed.
God blessed her, as He will all those who strive
To make another happy!

"Jesus Wept."

John xi. 35.

His sandalled feet were travel-stained,
His journey had been long,
And faintly on His staff He leaned,
The weariest of the throng.
But all-forgetful of Himself
Was that kind, heavenly breast;
Working for those He should redeem,—
The Saviour might not rest.

Grief was around the sepulchre;—
The little loving band
Were drawing nigh to Bethany,
And missed the greeting hand:
The ever-ready smile of love,
The tender, thoughtful care,
Came not as they were wont to do,
For Lazarus was not there.

The sisters tremblingly drew near,
Swayed by their mighty grief,
And many followers, gathering round,
Strove to impart relief;
But Mary, in her agony,
Pressed to the Saviour's side,
And said, "Lord, if Thou hadst been here,
My brother had not died."

He looked upon the stricken form
 With His all-pitying eye,—
Then at the friends who late had said,
 " Lord, let us also die !"
And over the Redeemer's soul
 A flood of anguish swept :
His spirit groaned beneath the load
 Of grief;—and " Jesus wept."

He did not weep when, fierce and strong,
 His enemies drew near ;
The " Crucify Him !" of the crowd
 Drew not a single tear.
The cruel scorn, the bitter taunt,
 His fervent spirit bore ;
Not for Himself that face Divine
 Its mournful aspect wore.

Why now these tears ? He knew a word
 Could bring the absent breath—
That Lazarus might smile again,
 For He could conquer death.
He knew that He would waken him,
 From this his transient sleep,
And that the life-tide would flow back—
 Then why did Jesus weep ?

He wept for sympathy with those
 Who bore the sufferer's part,
For human sorrow has such power
 To touch that mighty heart.
The " World's Salvation" could not see
 Grief upon those He loved—
Woe in the eyes that turned to Him—
 And He remain unmoved.

Jesus, we thank Thee for Thy tears;
For, when our hearts are sad,
We know Thou wilt not turn away,
But make the mourner glad.
And when our broken spirits faint,
And sorrows o'er us sweep,
Remind us, O all-tender Friend,
That Thou in love didst weep.

" What are the Wild Waves Saying?"

"The floods have lifted up, O Lord, the floods have lifted up their voice; the
floods lift up their waves."—Psalm xciii. 3.

THE voice of God is in the waves that wildly o'er us sweep,
The rough dark watercourses of affliction's mighty deep;
They speak to us in thrilling tones of that Eternal Power
Who "in the hollow of His hand" retains them every hour.
"What are the wild waves saying?"   Let us listen as they roll,
While their deep language solemnly finds entrance to the soul.

Ah! they have swept our friends away! How rapidly they fled
Before their rushing might into the region of the dead!
How vain our frantic eagerness to hold them as they fly!
Yet from the moving waters there is sent a kind reply:—
Blest are the dead who die in Christ, for they shall resting be,
When the earth melts "with fervent heat" and there is "no more sea."

Again the water-floods rise high, and from our loosened grasp
Have swept the life-long treasures which we held with fondest clasp,—
The comforts of our home fireside, the dazzling light of fame,
The favour of our fellow-men, the honour of our name;
And when we ask the reason why, the tempest wild replies,
" He speaks, and at His high command the stormy billows rise."

And yet again, with fearful force, the angry waters rush,
And now the spirit is subdued, and there is solemn hush;
The pulse is low, the cheek is pale, and faintly comes the breath,
And nature sinks in terror from the hov'ring shade of death.
But sweetly comes the Master's voice, " 'Tis I—be not afraid !"
Ye waters, "peace, be still;" for "here shall your proud waves be
    stayed."

"What are the wild waves saying ?" From the throne of God above,
Laden, they flow to us below, with messages of love ;
Yet, when the storms are beating and our spirits quake with fear,
'Tis sweet to look above and see the " Rock of Ages" near,
To hear our God say, " Hitherto, but now no further come,"
To feel the waves are bearing us yet nearer to our home.

The Past.

O! SWEET are the thoughts of the too-fleeting past,
Life's glorious sunshine, too brilliant to last;
Like soft-breathing harp-notes they gush through the mind,
These thoughts of those seasons now far, far behind.

When my spirit grows faint 'neath the hot, scorching beam,
'Tis pleasant to lave it in memory's stream,
And yet 'tis a feeling of exquisite pain—
This yearning to live it all over again !

The flower-clad greensward where gaily I roved,
The song of the streamlet my spirit so loved,
Those seats by the fire-side whence joyous and free
Rose the song and the laughter—so thrilling to me ;

The eyes that smiled on me, the dear lips that blessed,
The voices that cheered me, the kind hands that pressed,—
The thoughts of those pleasures remain with me yet;
They are past, they are past—but I cannot forget.

And the future looks gloomy and lonely;—yet stay!
What was it so deepened the joy of my way?
'Twas the presence and smile of my Heavenly Friend,
And He is unchanging—His love will ne'er end.

So I'll hope, and press onward. The future may bring
Less sunshine than gladdened the days of life's spring;
But I cannot be wretched, wherever I roam,
With the love of my Father, the sight of my home!

"Bless us, and make us Blessings."

SOFTLY through the fragrant air
Rises oft this earnest prayer,
Reaching to that throne above,
Unto Him whose name is love:—

Bless us, Father, as we bow;
Breathe thy peace-words o'er us now;
Make us happy, pure, and good,
Full of love and gratitude.

Make us blessings! Grant that we
Christ-like in our aims may be;
Making glad the weary heart,
Pointing to the better part.

Love and save us; make us shine
In Thine image, Lord Divine!
Help us while we linger here,
Meeter for a higher sphere.

"I will come again."

John xiv. 3.

ALL desolate, and trembling, and faint-hearted,
    O'er life's rough hills we roam,
Mourning that Christ our Saviour has departed
    Unto His glorious home!

For here the closest and the best communion
    Seems incomplete and dim :
Our spirits scarcely realize the union
    Between our souls and Him.

For, though He cheers the path that is so dreary
    With messages of love,
The strife and tumult make us very weary—
    We long to rest above.

And O! how sweet the promise He has given,
    That He will come again—
That this strong veil that parts us shall be riven,
    And ended all our pain!

Jesus is gone before and is preparing
    Seats in that " better land,"
That we His bliss and glory may be sharing,
    There—at our God's right hand.

" A little while " there is for us to linger ;
    A little work to do ;
" A little while " to watch that pointing finger
    That leads the desert through.

And then, His love in His own accents telling,
    Jesus will come again,
And take us with Him to that peaceful dwelling,
    For ever to remain.

O Friend above all others ! we are sighing
    To see and feel Thee here ;
Joyful beyond expression will be dying,
    If it but bring Thee near.

"Neither Thirst any more."

Rev. vii. 16.

No thirst for love ! " The heart's deep well " in heaven
    Is filled with holy, satisfying love ;
Such friendship as earth dreamed not of is given ;
    Affection is the atmosphere above.

No thirst for knowledge ! There the Highest teaches,
    And none are ignorant within His school ;
Each favoured student truths sublimest reaches,
    And O ! how kindly does that Teacher rule !

No thirst for honour ! Crowns of life immortal
    Already wreathe the conqueror's stainless brow,
All who have passed within that blessed portal
    Far, far excel the haughtiest monarch now !

No thirst for happiness!   The ransomed spirit
  Bathes ever in unutterable joy!
Those who have gained that blissful shore inherit
  Deep, lasting gladness, nothing can destroy.

No thirst! no thirst!   Earth's cisterns, dry and broken,
  Shall tempt the faint, parched pilgrim there no more;
Life's gushing fountain, with its wealth unspoken,
  Pours freely, constantly, its deep flood o'er.

O! while we tread earth's way, 'mid scenes distressing,
  And groans too often from our faint hearts burst,
How sweet to feel our aching feet are pressing
  On to that land where there is no more thirst!

"Jehovah Jireh!"

"THE Lord will provide," though the way that we tread
  Is so gloomy and rough that we sicken and faint;
Though the tempest and terror brood over our head,
  There's an ear that attends to the lightest complaint.

" The Lord will provide" in the day of our need,
  Though the cisterns of earth may be broken and dry,
Though a dearth should come over the land where we feed,
  And desolate sorrow and danger be nigh.

" The Lord will provide" when our friends have all flown,
  And the lips that have blessed us are silent and cold;
When we journey in darkness, uncheered and alone,
  There's a Friend whose kind hand will not loosen its hold.

" The Lord will provide," when the evening of life
    Throws its shadows of gloom o'er the narrowing way,
When heart and flesh tremble and fail in the strife,
    And nature is sinking in solemn decay.

" The Lord will provide" when the depths of the grave,
    With their darkness and nearness and dread, shall appal,
When death shall have stricken the arm that would save,
    And vanquished and weak in the conflict we fall.

" The Lord will provide," then, wherever we go ;
    Let us trust to His goodness and cling to His side,
And fearlessly travel life's road, since we know
    That all will be well—for " the Lord will provide."

" Cast me not away from Thy Presence."

Psalm li. 11.

O GOD, in mercy look on me ;
My spirit knows not where to flee ;
Yet in its grief I come to Thee—
    O, cast me not away !

Thou seest me full of woe and sin,
With fears without and guilt within ;
Yet only Thou canst make me clean—
    O, cast me not away !

My sinfulness must Thee offend,
I feel I grieve Thee without end ;
And yet Thou art my only Friend—
    O, cast me not away !

Unbounded mercy, Lord, is Thine,
Unbounded misery is mine ;
Yet in Thy depth of love Divine—
   O, cast me not away !

Around Thy cross my arms I fling,
Unto Thy gracious sceptre cling,
Thou ever pitiest suffering—
   O, cast me not away !

I long to see Thy smiling face,
I long to feel Thy kind embrace,
My Father, in Thy boundless grace—
   O, cast me not away !

Weary, and wretched, and defiled,
Yet am I still Thy loving child,
And art not Thou my Father mild ?—
   O, cast me not away !

O, bind me ever to Thy side,
And let me in Thy shadow hide,
And always at Thy feet abide—
   O, cast me not away !

The Mount of Olives.

"And he went as he was wont to the Mount of Olives."—
Luke xxii. 39.

MORE than earthly light and glory
  Rested on the mountain brow,
Hallowed by such sacred footprints,
  That a halo gilds it now—
    Such a Saviour
  On its flowery sod to bow !

There the tears of love and kindness
    Fell from those all-tender eyes ;
There the fervent supplications
    From those lips were heard to rise—
        God-like breathings,
        Wafted to the upper skies !

O ! to rest where He once rested,
    Press the turf His feet have pressed
Gaze upon those scenes so sacred,
    Were to be supremely blessed !
        On the mountain
        Where the Saviour knelt to rest !

But to be with Him it needs not
    We to Olivet repair !
Where our spirits turn toward Him
    In their longings—He is there,
        And will bless us
        'Mid the hallowed scenes of prayer.

The Language of the Cross.

"Bring thy sins and sorrows here."

LIFE'S burdens are pressing on thee,
    As thou toilest o'er the sod ;
Thou hast learnt some bitter lessons
    In the way thy feet have trod :
Thy portion is mixed with sorrow,
    Thy cup has brimmed with woe,
And a dark cloud hangeth o'er thee
    Where'er thy footsteps go.

And weighing upon thy spirit
  Is the heavy load of sin;
Its mark is on thy forehead,
  And its deep, dire curse within:
And thy heart is well-nigh broken,
  O'erwhelmed by its rushing tide;
Thou art bowed by its sad confusion,
  But knowest not where to hide.

Yet cheer thee, desolate-hearted,
  A haven of rest is near,
And a voice of music entreats thee
  To cast thy burden here.
It is far too large and heavy
  For thy sinking heart to bear;
O, drop it, thou heavy-laden,
  With the soothing breath of prayer.

O, faint one, do not tarry
  In the wild unceasing strife;
Come to the Cross! I'll give thee
  Forgiveness, joy, and life.
'Twill soothe the crushing sorrow
  Within thy bleeding breast;
Wayworn, and sad, and weary,
  Come to the Cross and rest.

The Saviour's Assurance.

"All power is given unto me in heaven and earth."—Matt. xxviii. 19.

CHEER thee, sufferer, cheer thee;
  For the weary couch of pain
No longer than He pleases
  Shall thy sinking form retain.

All power is with thy Saviour,
  And His hand is nerved by love;
He tenderly prepares thee
  For thy home with Him above.

Faint not amid temptations,
  Thou who art sorely tried;
There is a blessed shadow
  Where thy spirit may abide.
A loving Friend permits it,
  He can see that it is best;
All power to Him is given—
  He will give the weary rest.

Thou who with loving labour
  Yield'st thy services to Him,
Success is in His keeping,
  He can fill thy cup to brim.
O, fear not for the future,
  But betake thyself to prayer,
That a crown of bright rejoicing
  May soon be thine to wear.

If we are friends of Jesus,
  We need not fear the strife
That with hasty feet attends us
  All our journeyings through life.
Nay, e'en the waves of Jordan,
  In that last and trying hour,
Will not fill our souls with terror,
  For the Saviour has all power.

"What is Man, that Thou art mindful of him?"

Psalm viii. i.

SERAPHS at Thy footstool bend;
Strains from golden lyres ascend;
Myriads of immortals kneel,
Rendering homage that they feel.

Nature praises Thee, its God;
Flowers are smiling from the sod;
Birds are singing as they fly;
All things join the harmony.

Sun, and moon, and twinkling star
Tell how great Thy glories are;
And the green earth at Thy feet
Joins the chorus full and sweet.

Since Thy works all praise Thee thus,
Father, why such love to us?
Help us, Highest, every hour
To adore Thy matchless power.

Autumn Winds.

THE "sad Autumn winds!" How they mournfully sigh,
As now they are sweeping with eagerness by!
How wild are the voices they bear on the gale!
How startling the music that moves through the vale!

The "sad Autumn winds!" They are mourning that death
Passes swift through the land on the Winter's chill breath,
That the leaves and the flowers of the Summer must fade,
And all beautiful things in the cold earth be laid.

The "sad Autumn winds!" O! the shadows they fling
To my heart can a thousand remembrances bring
Of friends who have left me to journey alone,
Who will hear never more their deep murmuring tone.

The "sad Autumn winds!" They will not blow in heaven!
There Spring and its flowers are eternally given;
And those I have loved so will meet me again,
For ever in beauty and peace to remain.

Our Advocate.

"If any man sin, we have an advocate with the Father, Jesus Christ
the righteous."—1 John ii. 1.

"WE have an Advocate!" Before the throne
   He pleads, who, dying, gave Himself for us;
Who paid His life to win us for His own,
   And loves the deathless souls He purchased thus:
He is our Advocate who has been slain,
And surely Jesus cannot plead in vain.

"We have an Advocate!" Our weight of sin
   Does not exclude us from the Saviour's sight;
For they were sinners that He died to win,
   And those whom He has saved are His delight.
O, the immortal love of that kind Friend!
He will be faithful until life shall end.

" We have an Advocate!"   O, raise a song
  Of lofty praise to Jesus' healing name ;
Eternal honours will we give ere long,
  And through the vaults of heaven His praise proclaim.
Save us, Redeemer, in Thy mighty love,
Plead for us till we dwell with Thee above !

Longing for Home.

FATHER, how wearily,
Sadly, and drearily
    Time passeth on !
O! how my aching heart
Yearns from it all to part—
    Longs to be gone !

This, where I waiting stand,
Is not my fatherland—
    Is not my home.
Only a pilgrim here,
Over the desert drear
    Sadly I roam :

Wistfully turn my eyes
Up to my native skies—
    Up towards heaven.
When may I come to Thee ?
When shall these shackles be
    Suddenly riven ?

D

Here darkly grows my life,
Laden with sin and strife,
    Burdened with grief.
There all is holy peace,
There love will never cease—
    Joy is not grief.

Is not the angel-song
Sung by the happy throng
    Wafted to me?
And from the sapphire hall
Surely sweet voices call,
    " Come and be free!"

Father, Thou hearest me
Raising my heart to Thee—
    Longing for home:
Graciously speak to me,
Bid me from earth be free,
    Bid me to come.

Morning Thoughts.

" Cause me to hear thy loving-kindness in the morning."—
Psalm cxliii. 8.

When night disappears and the daylight is dawning,
    And peaceful repose has my spirit refreshed,
O God of the darkness! my cry in the morning
    Shall still be to Thee, who hast given me rest.

Each day with its duties and moments of sadness,
    I need Thee, O Father, to lighten my way,
To turn e'en the dread and the grief into gladness,
    To cheer with Thy kindness the newly-born day.

O, speak to me words of Thy mercy on waking,
 To nerve me to labour, or sorrow, or strife,
That so 'neath Thy smile I may always be taking
 The steps that will lead through the pathway of life.

And so will my journey be happiness giving;
 So will my constant thought turn unto Thee:
And O that I always to Thee may be living—
 Thou who art mighty, O, speak unto me!

"He that watereth shall be watered also himself."

Proverbs xi. 25.

LIVE not to thyself alone,
Thou who stand'st before the throne;
Selfishness should ne'er be thine,
Who hast breathed the life divine.

If thy God has blessed thee thus,
Give thy blessing unto us;
Let us share thy happy lot;
Freely give—withhold it not.

Let the drops of kindness fall
From thy spirit on us all,
And upon thy blooming flowers
God will send the copious showers.

Know thou canst not live alone,
Others' souls the power must own;
Ne'er thy drops of grace withhold;
God will bless a hundred-fold.

The Pleasant Service.

O! LIGHTLY on His servant's head
Our Master's kind commands are laid;
Love guides the firm directing hand,
And wisdom has the service planned.

He sympathizes with us still,
And gives us strength to do His will;
Knows we are weak and He is strong,
Nor will the o'erwhelming toil prolong.

O! pleasant is the work He sends,
Since He will call His servants friends;
Will bless us as we onward go,
And make our cup to overflow.

Then, Master, let us ever be
Devoted only unto Thee,
Obeying all Thy righteous laws,
Living and dying in Thy cause.

The Best Choice.

'TIS not for treasures of gold,
    With all they buy to be mine;
Riches too great to be told,
    In a casket of jewels to shine.

'Tis not a laurel of fame
    To bind in a wreath for my brow;
For honours to wait on my name,
    While mortals admiringly bow.

'Tis not for friends to abound
  And lure me with flattery's smile,
To press in their eagerness round,
  The tedious hours to beguile.

No! 'tis to God to retreat,
  And share in His mercy divine;
To sit at the dear Master's feet—
  Such choice in its wisdom be mine.

The Grateful Retrospect.

"Because thou hast been my help, therefore in the shadow of thy
wings will I rejoice."—Psalm lxiii. 7.

ALL that my life has seen,
All that my lot has been,
  Darkness or light;
Seasons of deep distress,
Days of pure happiness,
  All have been right.

Difficult paths there were;
Many a lurking snare
  Compassed me round;
Yet, on this happy day,
Kneeling to praise and pray
  Still am I found.

And I am fain to own
Not by myself alone
  Have I thus stood:
Thou hast befriended me,
Blessed and defended me—
  Thou art so good.

Thou art my Father-God;
Every new step I trod
   Thou wast my Guide,
Loving me evermore,
Blessing me o'er and o'er,
   Still at my side.

What shall I render Thee
Who hast so tenderly
   Led me alway?
Father, I'll trust Thee still,
Waiting Thy holy will,
   Through the new day.

Under the shadowing
Of Thy Almighty wing
   I will rejoice.
O, through the future be
All Thou hast been to me;
   This is my choice.

Alone.

ALONE, alone!   Life's seasons are declining;
   Surely the sunset draweth very nigh!
Weary and sad I chant my low repining,
   While none to pity or to scorn is by.

Alone, alone!   Thick darkness gathers round me;
   My spirit trembles in the dreadful shade;
O, bitter is the sorrow that has bound me,
   Crushing the weight that on my heart is laid.

Alone, alone! This fiery, deep emotion
  Looks all in vain to find some fitting shrine;
This yearning heart, this passionate devotion,—
  There's nothing here round which it can entwine.

Alone, alone! In many a happy dwelling
  Bright swimming eyes into each other gaze,
And rosy lips most thrilling tales are telling;
  While I am weeping out the long, long days.

Alone, alone! The choral song is flowing
  From many a heart all radiant with love-light,
And beaming faces are with rapture glowing;
  While I am desolate this cheerless night.

Alone, alone! O God, how passing dreary
  To lonely hearts life's journey may become!
Is there no haven for the sad and weary?
  For wretched ones is there no tranquil home?

Alone, alone! O Thou who lov'st me ever,
  I almost feel Thee bending o'er me now;
Hast Thou been watching all this vain endeavour
  At human shrines this deep full heart to bow?

Alone, alone! O Holiest, receive me;
  All this wild creature-love forgive, forgive;
Pardon the heart that must so often grieve Thee;
  Love me, my Saviour, or I cannot live.

"Go in Peace."

Luke vii. 50.

O HOLY, blessed Saviour! Now and ever
 Speak to our fainting, trembling spirits thus :
Those words which from our hearts all fears will sever,
 In Thy great tenderness, breathe over us.

Speak them whene'er our halting feet may linger
 At the first step of the untrodden way;
When dimly we can see Thy guiding finger,
 O, speak these tranquillizing words, we pray.

Speak them whene'er, in silent reverence bending,
 We seek to hold sweet intercourse with Thee.
Prepare us life's engagements to be tending,
 With spirits from the world's defilement free.

Speak them whene'er with kindred hearts we gather,
 'Mid greeting tones and thrilling looks of love;
Give us Thy presence, then, O heavenly Father,
 And bless us with these peace-words from above.

And whisper them at last, O Saviour tender,
 In the dim twilight of this life's decline ;
Calmly and trustingly we then will render
 To Thy dear hands the spirits that are Thine.

The Night Lamp.

"We have also a more sure word of prophecy; whereunto ye do well that ye take heed, as unto a light that shineth in a dark place, until the day dawn, and the day-star arise in your hearts."
—2 Peter i. 19.

DARK is my journeying;
Storm-clouds their shadows fling :
 Star of my God !
Thanks that thy blessed light
Shines through the shades of night
 Over the sod !

Gloom spreadeth over me,
Solemnly, silently,
 Sunless and dark ;
But thou art shining here,
Making it disappear,
 Guiding my bark !

Dangers are all around,
Torrents and crags abound,
 Yet I am safe !
Storms are not tossing me
Over the blackened sea,
 Like a dead waif !

No ! I am pressing still,
On, up the narrow hill,
 Still toward home.
Soon will its towers be seen,
Soon shall I enter in,
 Never to roam !

Surely the future span
Cannot be darker than
  Paths I have trod.
Thanks that thy blessed light
Shines through the shades of night,
  Lantern of God!

"He restoreth my Soul."

As I walk through the path where my Father is guiding,
 How oft do I quit my firm hold of His hand!
How I wander from mercies which He is providing,
 To roam by myself through the dangerous land!

How oft the cool waters of life's crystal river
 Flow on in their sweetness untasted by me!
How seldom are thoughts of the bountiful Giver
 Suggested by all the kind gifts that I see!

And yet, when I leave Him, and mourn it in sadness,
 With pardoning love "He restoreth my soul;"
He breathes the soft words that suffuse me with gladness—
 The words that can tempests of passion control.

O! sweet is the thought that He never will leave me,
 Though faithless too often my heart is to Him:
O heart of deep love! would I never might grieve Thee
 Till these eyes with the death-film were dreary and dim!

The Pleasant Path.

"Her ways are ways of pleasantness, and all her paths are peace."

YES, a pleasant way is the way to God :
The flowers are springing about the sod,
The Sun of Righteousness shineth still,
And the fountain of life sends its little rill ;
And still, as the travellers wend along,
Rise the sweet notes of the pilgrim's song.

There are shady bowers where the weary rest,
And comforting words for the sad opprest,
Joy for the mourning in Zion's way,
Gladness of heart through the long bright day ;
And sweetly over the pilgrims rise
The balmy zephyrs from Paradise.

Then come with the buoyant step and heart ;
From the grovelling pleasures of earth depart.
Holier joys are awaiting thee,
Perfect in immortality !
Come with us through the pleasant way,
Nor longer 'mid fading treasures stay.

The Hallowed Spot.

"The place whereon thou standest is holy ground."

JOY to thee, Christian ! Thy dwelling is holy !
He who is holiest standeth by thee ;
Ground He has trodden is consecrate wholly ;
Sacred indeed must thy dwelling-place be.

Joy to thee, Christian! God is beside thee
 Nothing can touch thee to injure thee now
Sinners may scoff, and thy foes may deride thee,
 But thy Father can make all these enemies bow.

Christian, be careful! The ground thou art treading
 Must only be trodden with reverent feet;
Think of the light which the Highest is shedding;
 Lowliness deep for His worship is meet.

Bow thee then, Christian, and watch the bush burning:
 Listen! 'tis God who is speaking to thee!
O! when to the world and its duties returning,
 Pray that thy life from its sin may be free.

Come to the Cross.

COME! while thy youthful feet are lightly bounding
 Through the soft path where fragrant flowerets spring;
While the green hills and valleys are resounding
 With the rich song thy lips in gladness sing.

Come! while the low and tender words of blessing
 Fall like sweet notes of music on thine ear;
While those who love thee to thy side are pressing,
 And thy free heart knows not the pang of fear.

Come! while the future looks all bright with pleasure,
 And the fair sun shines in a cloudless sky;
While sorrow has not robbed thee of a treasure,
 Nor from thy happy spirit forced a sigh.

Come to the cross of Jesus in thy gladness,
It has a charm to make thee happier still;
Come! in the darkest season of thy sadness,
When thickening sorrows shall thy faint heart fill.

Come! while thy life is overcast with sorrow,
And o'er thee threatening clouds are hanging low;
While with deep terror watching for the morrow,
Lest it should bring thee deeper, bitterer woe.

Come! while the evening shades are round thee falling,
And day is drawing to an early close;
When soft, low voices are thy spirit calling,
And thou art hastening to thy long repose.

Come! when the fairest lights of earth are fading
In the mysterious darkness of the grave,
When death thy chilly brow and cheek is shading,
And thou art called to breast cold Jordan's wave.

Come! in *all seasons* to the cross of Jesus
And learn the thrilling story of His love;
'Twill cheer and sanctify, refresh and ease us,
Fit us for life on earth and rest above.

Walk.

WALK in the morn, when the birds' rich notes
Triumphantly burst from their tiny throats;
Walk in the midst of the bustling day,
When busy scenes are around thy way;
Walk in the calm, sweet sunset hour,
When the world seems like a shady bower.

Walk in the country—the whispering leaves,
The fragrant meadows, the golden sheaves,
The clear blue sky, and the flower-clad sod,
Will ever tell of the love of God.
Go! learn sweet lessons by walking there,
Amid nature's pictures so sweet and fair.

Walk by the side of the mighty sea,
As it rolls in its glory, so wild and free:
Its bounding billows and restless waves,
And the hidden depths of its darkened caves,
Have voices to speak of that God to thee,
In whose mighty hand is the wild, wild sea.

Walk in the city, and kindly scan
The speaking face of thy fellow-man;
Thou wilt see the traces of world-wide care;
Each has his burden of grief to bear:
But a brother's eye appeals to thee,
And a brother's heart needs sympathy.

Walk, yes, walk, and ever raise
Thy heart to heaven in songs of praise—
Praise, that this world is so fair and bright—
Praise, that thou livest in such delight—
Praise, that the brightest joys here given
Are dark to the bliss of thy home in heaven!

Let us tell Jesus.

"And went and told Jesus."—Matt. xiv. 12.

Ah! it was well for those woe-stricken friends
    To tell the Saviour of their crushing grief;
To go to Him whose sympathy ne'er ends,
    And supplicate His pity and relief.

And 'twill be well for us to go to Him
With all that makes this life of ours grow dim.

Let us tell Jesus—when the friends we loved,
   Too well, perchance, for things of mortal birth,
By death, or change, or exile are removed,
   And far less bright becomes our home on earth:
Let us tell Jesus, for His tender love
All human friendship is so far above.

Let us tell Jesus—when life's weight of care,
   With all its toils and duties, seems too great
For weak and fragile ones like us to bear,
   No arm but His can fit us for the weight;
And, when it wearies us, how sweet to rest
And lose it all on the Beloved's breast!

Let us tell Jesus—when around our way
   Darkness and difficulties seem to stand,
And, fearful lest our feet should go astray,
   We need some kindly voice, some guiding hand:
O, we could follow if He would but lead,
And He is always near in time of need.

Let us tell Jesus—when the shadows come
   And tell us eventide is drawing nigh:
If He but wait to bid us welcome home,
   We will not tremble, will not fear to die:
Let us tell Jesus all that may betide,
Till we shall dwell for ever by His side.

The Voice of the Trees.

Who has not felt that there are sounds of music in the trees?
Who does not love those wild wood-notes struck by the fitful breeze?
Whose spirit has not thrilled with awe amid the mighty rush
Or melted into tenderness beneath the sudden hush?
They are God's temples, and they all speak solemnly of Him,
Throughout the day's majestic reign, or in the twilight dim.
'Tis well to gather 'neath their roof, and 'mid their organ-peal,
To breathe the deep emotion which our burdened spirits feel.
'Tis well to listen for God's voice upon our bended knees,—
To take, as from His kindly hand, the teaching of the trees.

Along a shaded avenue, one calm, still summer's day,
A pale and thoughtful-looking boy was resting from his play,
When suddenly it seemed as if he felt an angel's wing,
And his young heart was strangely stirred by the unwonted thing.
The leaves were whispering to him that God was very near,
And so he knelt and prayed, "Speak, Lord, and let Thy servant hear."
Men told him he had wildly dreamed in that mysterious time,
And that his fragile frame would sink beneath a burning clime;
But with mild eye and voice he woos the dark-browed group to heaven;
He's working out the mission that beneath the trees was given.

Night's pall hung o'er the sleeping earth, and autumn's mournful sighs
Swept through the shivering branches, and awoke their piercing cries.
A quick impatient step trod o'er the leaves that lay in death,
And burning thoughts came rushing up with that short laboured breath;
And as the youth walked madly on, he said, with flashing eye,
"These trees, what mighty power they have—but what a worm am I?"
There came a whisper low, but deep, in that most fearful hour;
It told him that to wisdom's page belongs the highest power;
It pointed him to science, and he trod its hill-side o'er,
And men were taught and nations blest through the wild forest lore.

A man with stern and frowning face, and dark and sullen mien,
Stood caring nothing for the storms of that wild wintry scene ;
Yet something in those branches soothed the tempest in his breast,
And made him long for pardon, and for happiness and rest.
All faltering were the steps he took to his deserted home,
From which with harsh and angry words he had been wont to roam,
A timid face looked up to him : it was enough—his heart
Beat against hers with love once more, and healed the torturing smart.
Their sacrifice of praise that night with deepest joy was fraught,
For the sweet happiness the trees had in their lessons taught.

Another trod with measured step along the leafy aisle ;
A calm repose was at his heart, and on his lips a smile.
Prosperity athwart his course had thrown its brilliant light,
And every passing day appeared to bring him fresh delight.
Yet, as he mused beneath the trees, and saw that even they
Were no exception to the rule of general decay,
His heart uprose in earnestness to Him who dwells on high ;
"Lord, to Thy other blessings add a readiness to die."
Ah ! 'twas a necessary prayer, for soon there came a blow
That hushed that manly, throbbing heart, and laid the strong one low.

Yes ! priceless are the lessons which the dear old forests teach :
Let us go forth beneath the shade, and listen while they preach ;
And let us garner all their lore into our heart's recess,
Assured that He who speaks through them will every sentence bless.
They teach us far from earth's damp sod aspiringly to rise,
To let our hands, and heads, and hearts turn upward to the skies ;
For He who takes such care of them, with rain, and sun, and air,
Will bless the hearts that trust in Him with far more tender care.
Let us go forth into the fields amid the scented breeze,
Asking our Father oft to send sweet lessons through the trees.

I am Home!

The last words of a dying Christian.

I AM home! I've arrived at my sweet home at last,
And the cold swelling waves of the river are past;
My eyes are unclosing that late were so dim;
O! where is my Saviour? I long to see Him.

I am home! I am home! All my trials are o'er;
I shall labour, and suffer, and sorrow no more;
I shall slake my hot thirst at the clear crystal fount,
And peacefully rest on the heavenly mount.

I am home! I am home! O! the wonderful light—
The radiant beauty that bursts on my sight!
And there are the streets and the temples of gold—
I've heard of them oft, but the half was not told!

I am home! I am home! An angelical band
Has a welcome for me in my dear fatherland!
This robe and this crown are they really for me?
And are they the friends of my youth that I see?

I am home! I am home! and again I am young;
O! give me a harp that its notes may be strung;
O! teach me the music that floats through the air:
I dreamed not that heaven was so brilliant, so fair!

I am home! I am home! and my Jesus is here—
O! spirits immortal, make room for me near;
He loved me, He led me: O! now let me come
And lie at His feet—I am home! I am home!

"God be Merciful unto us, and Bless us."

At the birth of early morning,
When a gay song greets the dawning;
When the noontide sun is shining,
And the toiler is repining;
When the busy daylight closes,
And the weary head reposes ;
When the moon her watch is keeping,
And the world beneath is sleeping,
And the night's dark fold shall press us,
God be merciful, and bless us!

When our friends are kindly smiling,
All the pleasant hours beguiling ;
When they one by one are leaving,
Dying, changing, or deceiving ;
When the sky is bright above us,
And all nature seems to love us ;
When the clouds are darkly lowering,
Heavy drops of sorrow showering,
And the woes of life oppress us,
God be merciful, and bless us!

When along our path we're singing,
And the flowers are freshly springing,
And our feet are lightly going,
Where the water-brooks are flowing ;
When temptations throng around us,
Danger and distress surround us ;
When our hearts with grief are wailing,
And our mortal strength is failing;
When disease and death possess us,
God be merciful, and bless us!

A Day.

ONLY a day—one little day!—
　Full half its hours were wasted;
We trifled in its morning prime,
　Forgetting how it hasted.
The day had passed full oft before,
　Nor brought us much of sorrow,
And at its close we had not grieved.
　For soon would come "to-morrow."

Only a day—we ate and laughed,
　And talked about the weather,
Lounged easily upon our chairs,
　And played and sang together;
Then worked or read a little while,
　According to our liking,
And scarcely thought upon the hours
　That one by one were striking.

Only a day—but near our home
　A hundred might be dying;
And many, many hundreds more
　In misery were sighing;
Starvation came to some that day,
　And suicide to others,
And ignorance and vice enchained
　More of our poorer brothers.

Only a day—but 'twas the last
　That ever came to many;
They shrieked aloud for helping friends,
　But were not heard by any.

Some dyed in deeper, blacker crime
Hearts that were well-nigh bursting,
And drank a poisoned draught, to see
If it would quench their thirsting.

Only a day—we might have helped
To stem the raging waters;
We might have blessed and comforted
Earth's wretched sons and daughters.
But surely through a few short days
Such things might be neglected;
And so we laughed and chatted on—
What more could be expected?

Toil and be Strong!

Toil and be strong! Within thy happy dwelling
How weariness and sadness o'er thee creep!
How, when the vesper song is softly swelling,
Thou lov'st to steal away from all, and weep!

How silently the dreaded shroud of weakness
Is wrapping in its subtle folds thy strength!
How does thy spirit bow itself in meekness,
Until thou'rt prostrate on the earth at length!

Yet rouse thyself, if thou wouldst soon be stronger;
It is in labour strength and power lie;
Arise and work, struggle a little longer,
Not till God bids thee is the time to die.

Toil and be strong! There's work enough before thee:
Stir the weak limbs, and nerve the fainting heart;
For He whose searching eye is ever o'er thee
Requires of each that he do well his part.

The Best Friend.

BEAUTIFUL words from the lips of One
Who is ever His people's cheering Sun!
Calmly they float o'er the troubled mind
As the zephyr's breezes, the summer's wind,
Easing the soul of its weight of care,
Hushing complaints in a holy prayer.

For they speak of a deathless love to me—
Of a better than human sympathy—
Of a friendship ever unchanged by years,
That deeper groweth 'mid grief and tears—
Of a godlike, infinite tenderness,
That when all is faded lives to bless.

And sorrow itself becomes almost fair,
With such a companion as He to share;
Loneliness cannot be sad and drear
With the angel-form of His presence near;
And blessed indeed must affliction be
That meets with such loving sympathy.

The pilgrim's walk through the vale of life
Is ever darkened by sin and strife;
But O! 'tis precious to have a Friend
Who will love and bless to the journey's end—
To feel that the aching head may rest,
And be gently soothed on the Healer's breast.

Holiest! O, be this Friend to us;
Sympathize, comfort, and bless us thus;
And till this toilsome life is o'er
Help us to love Thee and praise Thee more;
Spare us to meet Thee at home in heaven,
Where closer union with Thee is given.

The Glorified Redeemer.

O, for a single glimpse of Him upon the throne of light,
If it were not too radiant for weak and mortal sight!
O, for a moment nearer Him within that world above,
To see those flaming eyes dissolve in deep and God-like love!

How bright must heaven be that e'er is lighted up by Him,
The halo of whose shining brow no mists of earth may dim,
Whose beaming glance illuminates each fair and golden street,
And rests upon th' adoring head bowed lowly at His feet!

'Tis meet that many crowns should be upon His regal head,
He before whom such myriads their highest honours spread;
He who is Lord and King of nature, providence, and grace,
And worshipped by the happy ones within that holy place.

O, that I too might join them there, and share the glory now!
With love ineffable I'd place my crown upon His brow!
Yet, no; that honour were too great: if I might gain His seat,
I'd bow among the lowliest, and cast it at His feet.

Our Island Home.

God's blessing upon thee, dear land of my birth,
The brightest and fairest green spot of the earth;
The hearts of thy children are clinging to thee
In fond recollections, wherever they be.

What beauty there is in the blue of thy skies—
On the tips of thy hills that so gracefully rise—
In the fields and the meadows, and streamlets that glide—
The tint of the sunset—the swell of the tide!

And thou hast much wealth in thy noble of soul,
Who labour all evil to stem and control,
Who are willing to die for the weal of their land,
And lovingly, prayerfully, guarding thee stand.

O England! God bless thee, and make thee to shine
The fairest of earth, with these blessings of thine;
And still may thy children, wherever they roam,
Keep warm in their hearts this affection for home.

" Give us this Day our Daily Bread."

Matt. vi. 11.

GIVE us "*the bread that perisheth,*" O God!
    Thine are the air, the sunshine, and the shower:
Without Thy blessing fruitless is the sod,
    And vain all efforts are without Thy power:
'Tis by Thy hand Thy children, Lord, are fed;
O, " give us day by day our daily bread!"

Give us *the bread of love!* Hearts hungering
    Lie unconcealed beneath Thy pitying eye;
Thou seest the tendrils longing still to cling,
    Thou know'st the yearning thought, the hidden sigh
Thou art the source of all affection—give
The bread that makes it such a joy to live

Give us *the bread that is our spirits' need*—
   The kindling thought, the images sublime—
The power in nature glorious truths to read,
   And throw a halo round the things of time,
The mighty intellect, the expanding mind,
Give us, O Thou who art for ever kind!

And O, give us *Thyself—Thou Bread of Life!*
   For Thou alone hast power to satisfy;
Nought else can strengthen for the toil and strife;
   Without it we grow weak, and faint, and die.
Father! by Thee Thy children must be fed:
O, "give us day by day our daily bread!"

The Unknown Future.

"What I do thou knowest not now, but thou shalt know hereafter."
John xiii. 7.

THE things that are so painful here,
When earth's thick mist shall disappear,
Will 'mid our brightest blessings shine,
And show the Giver's love divine.

That future will a cause reveal
For every sorrow that we feel;
But here we cannot understand
The love that guides the Smiter's hand.

But patience yet a "little while,"
And He who seems to frown will smile;
In that "hereafter" of relief
Our hearts will bless Him for the grief.

Who are Around the Throne?

Who are around the throne?   Not those
  Who never knew a sorrow,
Who had no fears, nor pain, nor strife,
  Nor tremblings for the morrow;
Not those upon whose flower-clad path
  Earth's sun was ever shining;
Who never saw their precious things
  In death's embrace reclining!

Who are around the throne?   Ah, those
  Who oft were faint and weary,
To whom the world and all its scenes
  Were dangerous and dreary;
Whose hearts beneath a deep, deep grief,
  Unblessed, unhelped, were aching;
Who trod the path the Saviour trod,
  When friends were all forsaking.

Who are around the throne?   The tried,
  Who were by trouble driven,
For sorrow is the royal road
  That leadeth unto heaven.
O! welcome then the painful cross,
  With all its grief and anguish,
If there's a home above for me,
  When 'neath its weight I languish.

Not unto Us.

Not unto us, O Lord most high,
For we should fall wert Thou not nigh :
Our boasting would be all in vain ;
If Thou forsake we must be slain.

If ours should be the lighter sin,
Thou dost restrain the thoughts within :
Not in our weakness can we live ;
The needful strength is Thine to give.

Thou knowest best how, day by day,
We pass the dangerous hours away ;
And if the precipice be past,
Thine is the glory first and last !

Not unto us, O Lord, when death
Quiets the pulse and steals the breath ;
Thine shall the endless glory be,
For Thou alone canst set us free.

The Call of Samuel.

Night stole on Shiloh ! All the weary train
Of worshippers went out of God's high house
To rest.   The crimson sunset threw a flood
Of liquid glory o'er the ark of God,
Dwelling between the cherubim.   The gold
That overlay it richly did not seem
So beautiful as the deep glow that spread
Over the mercy-seat behind the veil !

Dim and mysterious grew tho sacred aisles,
And silent were the foot-falls of the priest,
And his loved boy-attendant—he who was
So early set apart for God. The lamp
Had not gone out when he lay down to sleep
In childish confidence. Awhile he thought
Of his loved mother in that far-off home,
How she had parted his fair clustering curls
With her own fingers—how the tears had gushed
Into her eyes at the last look, and how
Her pallid lips had quivered as they pressed
Fond kisses on his own. And then he dreamed
He was again in his own childhood's home,
Playing amid the trees.

                        Softly there came
Stealing upon his slumbers a low voice—
" Samuel! Samuel!" And the boy arose,
Shook off the weariness that wrapp'd him round;
And, pushing back his air with his white hand,
Ran unto Eli—" Here am I!"

                                It must
Have been a dream! And so he went again
As Eli bade him. Yet again that voice,
In its low accents—" Samuel! Samuel!"
Thrice did he hear it, and the boy looked grieved
That Eli should deny it. " Thou *didst* call,"
He said, " and here am I!" And then the priest
Perceived that God had called him; and he laid
His aged hand upon him as he said,
" Go, and lie down; and if He call again,
' Speak, Lord, for Thy servant heareth,' thou shalt say."
O! 'twas a solemn thing for that young boy
Waiting for God amid those holy courts,

Listening for what Omnipotence might say!
Again He came, and, as at other times,
He stood and called; and the young spirit went
Forth to his God in that close intercourse!
The morning came. A shade of sadness lay
On Samuel's countenance, and his young heart
Was heavy at the tidings he had heard ;
He shrank from meeting Eli, and went out
To open the Lord's house with trembling step.
O! it is sad to have to speak the words
That wound a heart we love! Yet when it is
A message from our God, we must not fear
To do His bidding.
     Samuel hid his face
Against that bursting heart, and told him all ;
And the old stricken man bowed down his head
In silent resignation—" 'Tis the Lord!
Let Him do all that seemeth good to Him."

Saturday Evening.

THE shades of evening softly fall,
 And silence reigns around ;
Saviour, as these last hours pass by,
 We would with Thee be found!

Thy hand has led us safely through
 The week's vicissitude ;
And now we lift our hearts to Thee,
 For Thou art kind and good.

We thank Thee for Thy mercies past,
  For life, and strength, and health;
Thy love is all our stay, O God!
  Thy smile is all our wealth.

We thank Thee for the Sabbath day;
  O may its moments be
Some foretaste of that blissful rest
  We hope to spend with Thee!

Keep Thou our thoughts, that in Thy house
  We serve the God we love;
And let us join the songs they sing
  Around Thy throne above.

O! spread Thy sheltering wing around,
  Till all these Sabbaths cease,
And we are safely landed where
  There is eternal peace.

The Night Cometh.

Thou'rt happy, little child, among the sunshine and the flowers,
Thy tiny feet are dancing through the cheerful morning hours;
Thou'rt laughing as they tell thee of a lamp to light thy way,
Thou think'st thou wilt not need it through the long, long summer
      day;
Thou seest not the shadows which the night ere long will cast,
But, little one, they'll hang above thy drooping head at last.

Thou'rt dreaming, thoughtful youth, of many happy hours in store,
Thou paint'st the future very bright with learning's wealthy lore,

Thy brilliant eye is gazing on the steep ascent to fame,
Thou'st vowed to gain its lofty height, and carve thereon thy name;
Thy lip is curled in scorn to those who talk of night to thee;
It is not yet the noontide hour—yet short thy day may be.

Thou thinkest not of sorrow's night, O thou of gentle brow!
It cannot come while those dear eyes smile tenderly as now;
A cloudless sun shines o'er the home his love so sweet has made;
Thou'rt clinging to thy noble oak, and resting in its shade:
But joy like thine is very short; O! kneel before 'tis gone;
Pray for a lamp to light thee through the night that cometh on.
And thou who'rt strong and healthy, in the height of manhood's
        prime,
Dream'st not how silently the hours are bringing evening-time;
Yet there are gathering shadows slowly creeping o'er thy way,
And whispers floating through the air speak of a closing day.
Thou'rt prudent in thy worldly aims—hast thou provision made
For the dark season coming on, when day and life shall fade?

Servant of God! Strange that to thee the night seems distant still,
When thoughts of its approaching should thine inmost spirit fill;
O! wake thy dormant energies, and let the startling tale
Spread through this world of carelessness on each careering gale.
Tell mortals that the night of death is quickly coming on;
They'll need the Gospel's light indeed when life's faint sun is gone.
Ah, yes! the long, dark, rayless night is coming to us all;
Around our homes, upon our hearts, its deepening shadows fall.
"O Sun of Righteousness, arise with healing on Thy wings,"
When o'er our trembling, shrinking forms its blackened shroud it flings.
And when the heavy hand of death falls on our failing sight—
O! take us to the cloudless land where there is no more night!

"Behold, a Door was opened in Heaven."

Rev. iv. 1.

WHAT is within the door ?   O, for a dream
Of that eternal city !   How the heart
Prays but for one short glance, in which to see
Glimpses of all its glory !   And the thought
That soars e'en to its portal fails at last,
For to our straining eyes that guarding door
Is not yet open.   But the favour'd John
Has left his record, and on that we base
Our expectations while we linger here
Waiting the signal to ascend to God.
Within that door there is the great white throne,
Its emerald rainbow round it.   Golden streets,
And founts of crystal water; jasper walls,
And gates of pearl, and paths of precious stones ;
And there are numbers which no man could count,
Of holy, happy spirits, patriarchs,
And prophets—men who waited long, and bore
Their witness for their God.   And there are some
Who lived and suffered silently, unknown
Upon the earth.   And some who came
From hot and scorching countries, on whose brows
Jesus has placed His mark.   Some, too, there are
Whose infant tongues just lisped His praise below:
And some familiar to our hearts, who went
From our embraces at the welcome call
Of the sweet voice they longed for.   Harps of gold
And palms of victory are in the hands
That grow not weary now ; and crowns of gold
Are theirs to cast before the Saviour's feet,

Who gave Himself for them.   And through the air,
Borne on their wings of light, the angels pass ;
And all with one accord join in the song
Of swelling Hallelujahs.

                              O! the joys
Of heaven tongue may not utter.   Yet, methinks,
Were the door opened now, I would not gaze
On all these glories, but would cast myself
Low at His feet whom I so oft displease :
For it were heaven indeed to see Him smile
Upon me—to throw off the weariness
And sin of earth, and feel that I were His
For all eternity!

Summer-time.

THE summer-time, the summer-time, how beautiful it seems!
The sun is glancing everywhere its strong and radiant beams ;
There's sunshine in the cotter's home, where everything is neat,
And sunshine in the palaces, and sunshine in the street.

The lark pours from its tiny throat its thrilling hymn at morn,
Uprising from its lowly nest among the waving corn ;
The nightingale is warbling forth its witching vesper song,
As twilight breathes away the day, that never is too long.

The flowers are sweetly smiling in the valley, on the hill ;
The weeping willows stoop to kiss the little laughing rill ;
There is a balmy fragrance in the scarcely-moving air,
The very wind is music, and there's beauty everywhere.

The little children skip and play beneath the shady trees,
Their sunny curls are blown about by every passing breeze ;
The labourer goes forth to toil, or rests at noon to dine,
And murmurs gratefully, " Bless God ! the harvest is so fine."

F

Yes, let us all bless God indeed, and wipe the heated brow ;
'Tis God that sends the summer-time, and we will praise Him now :
He clothes the world in beauty, makes our earthly home sublime,
While gladness fills our swelling hearts—bless God for summer-time!

———

ῼow will thou do in the Swelling of Jordan?

Jer. xii. 5.

WHEN sickness shall thy spirit bow,
And anguish rack thy heart and brow ;
When faintly throbs the pulse of life,
And flesh is failing in the strife,
And shorter grows the laboured breath—
How wilt thou bear th' approach of death ?

When those who love thee disappear,
And new strange sounds steal on the ear;
When the weak brain begins to swim,
And earth with all its joy grows dim,
And death is calling thee away—
How wilt thou bear that trying day ?

When Jordan's darkening waters swell,
And every billow tolls thy knell ;
When o'er thee creeps an icy chill,
And dread thy sinking heart shall fill—
While higher mounts the o'erwhelming wave—
And thou art dying—who will save ?

I will fear no Evil, for Thou art with me.

Psalm xxiii. 4.

THOUGH on the yielding shore I tread,
And tempests lower above my head,
Though the fierce tide is rising high—
Yet I am not afraid to die :

For Thou art with me—Thou whose power
Can shield me in the trying hour ;
And to Thy mighty hand I'll cling,
When the cold waves around me spring.

Speak to me in the swelling tide,
And in the rock's great shadow hide ;
O! let me feel that Thou art nigh,
And then I will not fear to die.

But when to Jordan's banks I come,
And see from thence my shining home,
Fearless I'll breast the rising wave,
Since Thou art with me, and wilt save.

Looking unto Jesus.

Heb. xii. 2.

"LOOKING to Jesus!"   At the opening year
   Sorrow and dread press on my sinking heart ;
The present is but dark, and still I fear
   The future will but bring the sufferer's part.
Weak is the spirit to endure alone—
Jesus, I raise my eyes unto Thy throne!

F 2

"Looking to Jesus!" On this New Year's day
  Sad memories a gloomy shadow fling;
Hopes that were bright have passed to swift decay;
  Hearts that have blessed me with their cherishing,
And joys that were too great for earth, are gone—
Saviour, I need Thee as I journey on.

"Looking to Jesus!" Duties cluster round,
  And calls to labour everywhere I hear;
Yet am I weak, and faint, and strengthless found,
  Unfitted for the struggle that is near.
Almighty Helper, let me lean on Thee;
Strength to the strengthless Thou dost love to be!

"Looking to Jesus!" Ever while I live
  I would be looking, Saviour, unto Thee;
All that Thy helpless child is needing give,
  Till from this earth the longing soul is free.
O! stay with me till life itself shall end;
Loving Redeemer, ever be my Friend!

The Appeal.

"Lovest thou me?"—John xxi. 16.

LOVEST thou Me? I have lived a life
Clouded by suffering, woe, and strife;
Have prayed whole nights on the cold, damp sod,
And rough and steep were the paths I trod;
My life and death were My love to thee,
Cheerfully given—and lovest thou Me?

Lovest thou Me ?   I have led thee far
Through the meads where the living waters are,
Have made thy journey with mercy bright,
Have kept thee safe through the darksome night,
Have made thy spirit from bondage free,
Have blessed thee ever—and lovest thou Me ?

Lovest thou Me ?   I am ever near,
With the watchful eye and the listening ear;
Thy faintest sigh and thy softest prayer
Are heard, and then I am with thee there;
Comfort and peace I have breathed o'er thee
In the day of storm—and lovest thou Me ?

Lovest thou Me ?   My blood has bought
Joys with eternal richness fraught—
A better home in the far-off land,
A seat of rest at My Father's hand;
Immortal life I have sought for thee,
A fadeless crown—and lovest thou Me ?

Lovest thou Me ?   When at last in heaven
The robe and the harp to My friends are given,
'Mid all that is holy, and bright, and fair,
And immortal, wilt *thou* be absent there ?
Will they shout the chorus of victory
While thou art silent—nor lovest thou Me ?

Lovest thou Me ?   I know thy heart
Will oft grow cold, and from Me depart;
I know thou wilt grieve thy Friend—and yet
I love thee still, and will not forget.
By all the depth of My love for thee,
Let thy spirit answer—lovest thou Me ?

The Response.

"Yea, Lord; thou knowest that I love thee."—John xxi. 16.

Loving Saviour! Thou canst see
How my spirit thirsts for Thee;
How I am unsatisfied
When I wander from Thy side;
How the dearest joys of earth,
Hours of thoughtfulness or mirth,
Cannot bring me happiness,
Unless Thou remain and bless.

All that Thou hast done for me
Binds my heart in love to Thee;
And Thy messages of love
Make me long to dwell above.
Thou hast washed me in Thy blood,
Thou art guiding me to God,
Pleading for me at His throne:
Saviour, I am all Thine own!

Yet my weak and faithless heart
Ever prone is to depart,
Unless Thou wilt keep me near,
Walking in Thy holy fear.
O, permit me not to stray
From Thy holy, narrow way;
Take my hand, and let it be
Clinging to none else but Thee.

Dear Redeemer! love me still;
Bend my spirit to Thy will;

Let me be Thy loving child,
While I tread this desert wild;
Lead me to that shining home,
Where temptations never come;
Folded in Thy arms I'll be
Ever, ever loving Thee!

Morning.

In the east the sun is shining
  On the golden grain;
Hark, the voice of duty calling
  Bids us rise again!

Angels o'er us have been watching
  Through the silent night;
Let us turn our thoughts to heaven,
  Blessing God for light.

And with undiminished ardour
  Let us forward go;
Hands, and head, and heart be **working**
  While we stay below.

Let us find some task completed,
  Something nobly done,
That shall earn a night's reposing
  At the set of sun!

All Right.

The late Capt. R. Petley, a few days before his death, said to a friend who was with him, "It is all right—the covenant is sure."

"ALL right!" And why? That a life well spent
Has brought an evening of calm content?
That the faithful walls of the memory
Are hung with pictures of charity?
That thoughts of righteous deeds well done
Have thrown a joy round the setting sun?
No; for the holiest deeds alone
For the sins of a moment could not atone!

"All right!" And why? That to him was given
The boon of wealth from the King of Heaven?
That partial judges have graced his name
With the laurel-wreath of a well-earned fame?
That loving eyes will bedew his bier
With grateful hearts and affection's tear?
No? for these are neglected all
When disease and death with their voices call.

"All right" that the promise of God is sure,
The love of the Saviour will still endure;
That his failing eyes o'er the water's foam
Can see the lights in his shining home;
That the angels with eager arms are nigh;
That the veteran is not afraid to die!
O that we, when our lives are past,
May say from the heart, "All right!" at last.

And there was very Great Gladness.

Nehemiah viii. 17.

JERUSALEM blazed in the autumn's clear sun,
And well-nigh the work of the captives was done;
And they gathered the branches of myrtle and pine,
And olive and palm with the flowers to entwine.

And they sat in the booths which with joy they had made,
While the breath of the myrtle perfumed the soft shade;
And the green trellis hung o'er the streets of their home,
And the temple looked fair with the wreaths on its dome.

When softly there pealed through the vistas all dim,
The sweet solemn strains of their tremulous hymn;
While the people fell down on the roofs that they trod,
And calmed their full hearts in the worship of God.

And the governor's voice rang majestic and high,
With his lofty brow bared to the deep azure sky;
And he read 'mid their sobs of God's goodness and love,
Till they gratefully pealed their glad anthem above.

And there came on the hearts that had lately been sad
Such blessings from heaven that they sang and were glad,
And their beautiful city re-echoed with joy,
For far were the foes that had sought to destroy.

They kept the long-slighted commands of their God,
Who had brought them safe back to their own belov'd sod;
His smile was upon them, once more they were free—
How kind and forgiving a God He must be!

The Countless Multitude.

"A great multitude which no man could number."—Rev. vii. 9.

THERE are bright angels! Round the flaming throne,
  Veiling their faces with their wings, they stand;
Those who ne'er shed a tear nor breathed a groan
  Assemble, clothed in light, at God's right hand,
Leading with lyres of more than human mould,
That song whose language mortal lips ne'er told.

And there are children! Those whose brows all pure
  Have early won the crown of fadeless light;
Who lived, but had no sorrows to endure,
  Whose little day was never quenched by night.
Ah! there are crowds of them in that bright world
Where the victorious banners are unfurled!

And there are saints who in the Saviour's blood
  Have washed their robes; and they are white as snow.
From life's drear journey and from death's dark flood
  A deep repose, a holy calm, they know.
Oh! how the voices of that rapturous throng
Swell through the arch of heaven the choral song!

Yet there is room! O pilgrim on earth's way,
  Say, whither are thy footsteps journeying?
Wilt thou not press toward that brightening day?
  Wilt thou not join the chorus that they sing?
O! 'mid that countless multitude to be,
Would be indeed a cloudless heaven to thee!

The Unseen.

" We endure, as seeing him who is invisible."—Heb. xi. 27.

THE mist and darkness deepened o'er that man of threescore years,
And scarce the enduring spirit could keep back the scalding tears
As he beheld his treasured things in desolation lie,
And still lived on, and lived alone, through days of agony.
Yet from the trembling lip there came no passionate complaint,
No murmuring from the heart that grew so worn, and sick, and faint;
For there were unseen arms around, supporting him through all,
A more than angel form of love that would not let him fall.

A mother watched the fading of her own and only child :
"O ! spare her to my clinging heart," was the entreaty wild.
The mother had to check the fond, but wearying caress,
For still the loved form wasted, and the hope grew less and less.
Yet on that bleeding heart was laid a mighty healing hand,
And the rebellion fled like mists at His Divine command ;
There came a deep, unearthly peace, and she was heard to tell,
With chastened, trusting utterance, " He doeth all things well."

And she who felt with every pain and each decreasing breath,
That, walking side by side with her, was the dark monster Death,
Smiled sweetly, as the trying hour, with all its dread, drew nigh,
And heavenward, 'mid the suffering, raised her dim and languid eye.
" I fear not, I am not alone," with feeble voice she said ;
" Th' Invisible is here ; on Him I lean my weary head.
He strengthens me amid it all"—the voice was hushed—she slept ;
But the Supporter took her home, and soothed the hearts that wept.

O, God ! Thy feeble children's meed of agony is sure ;
And from Thy hand alone must come the power that can endure.
We see Thee not amid the gloom, and yet our thanks we give,
That evermore Thou givest us the strength through all to live.

O! while the wintry hurricanes around our spirits roar,
Let us but feel Thee near us, and the danger will be o'er.
In life or death Thy unseen hand shall our protection be—
O, meeten for the time when we may ever gaze on Thee.

Ministering Spirits.

CHRISTIAN! thou canst not be alone—thy onward path may seem
Dark, difficult, and all uncheered by sweet affection's beam;
Thou may'st feel lonely 'mid the crowd, who all are strange to thee,
May'st long for human friends, and love, and earthly sympathy;
Yet dream not that thou art alone, for ever by thy hand
Are visitants too pure for earth sent from the spirit-land.

Christian! tread softly, for to thee each spot is holy ground;
Seraphic forms and angel-wings are floating all around:
Bright messengers of mercy come to cheer thy passage home,
To bless thee, guard thee, guide the feet that otherwise would roam;
They come with thrilling messages sent by a Father's love,
And fan thy brow with breezes cool borne gently from above.

Christian! care less for earth, and pray to live as angels live;
Strive to commune with them, nor crave for joys the world can give;
Entreat thy God to make thee pure, that so thou mayest bless,
E'en as the seraphs do, this land of sorrow and distress;
So shall their mission be thine own, so shalt thou take thy place
In the same cloudless land, and gaze on the Redeemer's face.

Forget not God,

"Beware that thou forget not the Lord thy God."—Deut. viii. 11

Fair is the sun above thy head;
And the flowers around thy feet
Are blossoming fresh and beautiful,
And shedding a fragrance sweet;
Blessings are scattered athwart thy way,
And returning morn and eve
Find thee ever with some new joy,
Bearing the word, " Receive."
O! do not forget who giveth all—
With songs of praise at His footstool fall.

"Do not forget me," thy friends have said,
And thy fond and yearning heart
Beareth them ever some thoughts of love,
Though miles and years should part;
But if not in vain the pleading lips
And the voice of affection be,
Surely the Highest deserveth more
Than a passing thought from thee.
Child of His love! remember Him
Whose care and kindness life's chalice brim,

Forget not God! Each blade of grass,
Each finely-pencill'd flower,
Each murmuring rill, each singing bird,
And each bright and fleeting hour,
Tell of Him to the thoughtful mind,
In language pure and deep,
Whose tender, skilful, mighty hands
Safely creation keep.
Bow thee, O man, on the velvet sod,
And with grateful spirit acknowledge God.

Forget not God in the opening morn,
  Or the stilly evening's close ;
When thy busy brain is working on,
  Or thy wearied limbs repose ;
If pleasure beam o'er the gladsome path,
  Or the night of sorrow come,
Remember Him who will ever be
  His people's rest and home.
Gratefully think of the pathway trod,
And for all its blessings forget not God.

The still small Voice.

How through the twilight dim,
Like a low vesper hymn,
  Whisperings come ;
Raising the burdened thought,
Often with sorrow fraught,
  Up to our home !

One by one, over us,
Dreams that are glorious
  Silently spread ;
Breezes from Paradise
Float o'er the aching eyes,
  Rest on our head.

O ! it is sweet to be
Thus from our labour free,
  Low on the sod ;
Earnestly listening
For tidings thou shalt bring,
  Voice of our God !

The Unchanging.

"With whom is no variableness, neither shadow of turning."—
James i. 17.

This is a world of change! All things are dying,
  And those most precious are the first to fall!
Life's flow'rets beautiful are early lying
  Where dark decay has spread its funeral pall.

Change dims the eye that looked upon us brightly;
  Freezes the hearts that made us rich in love;
Change spoils the tones that speak to us so lightly;
  Ah! but it touches not the Friend above!

No change in Him! Coldly our hearts are beating,
  And there are seasons when we love Him not;
But tender still will be the Saviour's greeting,
  However changed or dark may be our lot.

Unchanged, unchanged! We bless Thee in our gladness,
  Dear Friend of sinners, who hast loved us so!
O, bind us to Thee in our hours of sadness,
  And linger near us every step we go.

The Hope set before us.

Heb. vi. 19.

Rest! when the labours of life are o'er,
When the free, glad spirit shall upward soar;
Peace! o'er the weary heart to steal,
While the ransomed ones adoring kneel;
Joy! that no withering storms decay,
When the things of earth shall have passed **away.**

A home! where everything speaks of love,
Tranquil and safe in that house above ;
A crown! of pure and unchanging gold,
That e'en through eternity grows not old ;
A robe! of beautiful, spotless white,
Dazzling and rich in the heavenly light !

The *friendship of myriads of holy men,*
Perfect and free from all tarnish then ;
The *love of angels* for ever there,
'Mid all that is sacred, and glad, and fair ;
The presence of Jesus, whose smile will be
Lasting and bright as eternity !

O, let us quicken our tardy feet—
Be our progress thither more blithe and fleet ;
Light is glancing upon the road,
And each step brings us nearer God !
" Onward and upward " our watchword be,
Till the gates of our beautiful home we see !

Thou who hast gone to prepare our place,
How are we longing to see Thy face !
Help us life's difficult hills to climb,
Looking beyond the events of time ;
Let the hope set before us still cheer our way,
Till the darkness closes in deathless day !

The Useful.

THEY are not great alone who live to do some *mighty* deed,
Who listen not to sorrow's cry unless when *millions* plead;
Life's duties gather silently along the lone roadside,
And Christ-like spirits will nct wish for scenes of wealth and pride.
They are the *really useful* who, with humble, reverent heart,
Unseen by earth's admirers, seek to do their secret part.

Applauding lips and flattering smiles may fascinate too well,
But praise from multitudes will cause the weak, vain heart to swell;
But better than the fading flowers which numbers round may fling,
Would be the Saviour's smile upon some lowly offering.
The "cup of water in His name" may bring His blessing down
More richly than the lofty deeds that win a world's renown.

The cooling touch that stays awhile one painful throbbing smart,
Or nerves to calm endurance still a faint and sinking heart;
The look of gentle warning that will check a sinful deed;
The lips that breathe the word of love which is the spirit's need;
The tones which rouse the nerveless soul to rise at duty's call—
O, "He who sees in secret" will in love regard them all.

Then cheer thee, lowly worker—though the world regard thee not,
There is an Eye that notes thee, and will bless thy humble lot.
Press forward to the rest that will be thine when time is past,
Nor weary of thy silent work; for know thy God at last
Will "openly reward thee"—and methinks 'twere sweet to be
Partaker in the welcome He will give to such as thee!

"Rejoice in the Lord."

Phil. iv. 4.

REJOICE in the Lord! There is light in the dwelling
  And peace in the spirit where Christ is the guest;
And surely the chorus might always be swelling
  Around the blest threshold which Jesus has pressed.

Rejoice in the Lord! He will scatter the sadness
  That broods o'er the sanctified home of His friends;
And days as they pass will be radiant with gladness,
  Where prayer from the family altar ascends.

Rejoice in the Lord! The fresh flow'rets are springing
  In fragrance and beauty to gladden thy way;
And the Father of mercies His largess is flinging—
  New tokens of love for each newly-born day.

Rejoice in the Lord! He is tenderly leading
  Each step that His wisdom requires thee to take;
And He will supply all the strength thou art needing,
  Who loveth for ever and will not forsake.

Rejoice in the Lord! There is joy for thee ever,
  If thou in thy life-time belongest to Him;
A bond—all of love—which no changes can sever,
  A sun o'er thy head which no storm-cloud can dim.

Rejoice in the Lord! He awaits thee in heaven,
  With myriads who made His light service their choice;
And shortly the robe and the crown will be given
  To thee! Then, believer, O! always rejoice!

The Hour of Evening Prayer.

Softly the daylight faded. The red sun
Sank gently down behind the gold-tipped hills ;
The evening breeze sighed soothingly among
The quivering forest leaves. The choristers
Which we call lowly, and look down upon
As detrimental to the summer-time—
The grasshoppers and gnats—unwearily
Poured forth their joyous music ; but the tired cattle
Sought the shade, and rested. The clouds
Floated on gracefully, and softly laid
Their coverlid above the wearied earth.

It was the hour for rest, and intercourse
With the unslumbering One, whose skilled hand makes
"Th' outgoings of the evening to rejoice."
'Twas sweet to see how many, in this time
Of soft, subduing quiet, turned their thoughts
And raised their spirits to the Infinite,
And prayed before the universal shrine
God has erected everywhere.

The fair-haired child,
Clasping its tiny hands, its bright blue eyes
Closed, meekly knelt beside its mother's knee,
And lisped the simple prayer her lips had taught
For the protection of the children's God.
Whose eyelids never droop.

The maiden sought
Her room, made holy by the sacred thoughts

G 2

And nameless yearnings under which her soul
Had often trembled; and then, throwing back
The shining tresses, laid her thoughtful brow
Upon the sacred page her kindling eye
Had been perusing; poured the gushing fount
Of passionate emotion at His feet
Who reads the heart's deep mysteries. For herself
She asked for holiness, and purity
Of life and conduct—that her days might be
A faint reflection of His days in whom
Was found no guile; and then, in softer tone
And deeper earnestness, besought of God
Blessings for all her loved ones.

　　　　　　　　　The young man
Folded his arms across his throbbing heart,
And watched with flashing eye the darkening heavens,
Till, breaking suddenly his joy-tinged dreams
Of future fame and greatness, raised his brow,
Flushed with a high resolve, and fervently
Prayed to the Infinite that he might be
God's honoured messenger, and make the world
Better and holier for his stay therein.
His pleading was not quickly o'er; for when
The stars looked down and smiled, his manly tone
Rose high in the still air—"O Father! Friend!
Place me among the truly great, e'en those
Whom Thou mak'st good!"

　　　　　　　　　The mother softly stole
Into the silent chamber, where the light—
The "last red light" of the departing day—
Tinged with its glorious beauty the soft locks
Of all her cherub children. She watched them,

Hushing her breath for very joy, until
The fount of love within her yearning heart
Came gushing up, and well-nigh overflowed.
And then she knelt, and poured its deep tide forth
In earnest wrestlings for the privilege
Of polishing her gems, to sparkle in
The Saviour's coronal.

The aged man
Leaned, tremblingly, upon his time-tried staff,
And, picturing the everlasting hills,
Toward which his worn feet tottered, where were all
In youth he loved so deeply, breathed a prayer
For blest re-union in the spirit-land.
And there were companies—

Whole families
Gathered around the altar, and sent up
A vesper sacrifice.

A little band
Met 'neath a low, but consecrated roof,
To crave a blessing.

And the multitude
With blended voices sang, "Glory to Thee,
My God, this night."

And there were couples, too,
Whose spirits grew too happy for this world,
Who knelt and poured the deep impassioned tide
Of feeling forth, in the sweet voice of prayer.

Earth may have many scenes of grief and strife;
Yet while the sunset comes, with its soft hours
And hallowèd emotions, let us bless
Our God for making it so beautiful.

A Glimpse of Heaven.

O FOR a glimpse of heaven! My spirit longs
  For but one glance at the fair fatherland!
My straining ear would catch the thrilling songs
  So sweetly warbled by the white-robed band.
This earth, with all its joys, is incomplete;
"I should be satisfied" at Jesus' feet.

Around my Saviour shining seraphs bow,
  And some I loved (how well!) are with them there,
Crowns of immortal life upon each brow,
  And on their faces not a trace of care.
Joy "heart of man hath not conceived" is given—
O! if I could but be with them in heaven!

A glimpse of heaven! No clouds athwart its sky!
  No fading flowers, where it is always spring!
No aching hearts, no tear, no frown, no sigh!
  No faltering voice to mar the strains they sing!
No weary feet or heart, no throbbing head!
No mourning over precious treasures fled!

And O! *to be with Christ!* Ever to lie
  Sweetly upon that loving Saviour's breast!
Drinking deep gladness from His beaming eye,
  And being full of love and peace and rest.
When, when, dear Jesus, shall the call be given?
When may I go and live with Thee in heaven?

Fireside Poetry.

A GROUP of little children sat beside the cheerful hearth,
And like sweet strains of music rose the sounds of childish mirth ;
And one on whose broad brow were stamped the lineaments of thought
Rich treasures from the Bible mine in simple language brought ;
The rosy lips were parted, and the undimmed eyes grew bright,
And all those little beating hearts were swelling with delight.
It was a lofty intellect thus bending to their ken—
Methinks to angel-eyes he ne'er had been so great as then.

A youth was parting from the friends that "clustered round his home,"
Life's busy din was calling him 'mid sterner scenes to roam ;
But O! those clinging arms, those eyes lit with such pleading love,
Will be to him as well-trimmed lamps, lighting his steps above.
The tempter's voice may tell him that the paths of sin are fair,
But in his heart will ever be thoughts of that fireside prayer—
Thoughts of those dear unselfish ones that felt so much for him,
Who with their gentleness and love oft made joy's cup to brim.

There were two loving hearts—but each was swayed by passion's
    storm,
With crimsoned cheek and flashing eye, and proudly straightened
    form ;
And angry, scornful words were passed, from white lips quivering,
And hearts were aching with the wounds loved hands were poisoning.
Surely it was an angel-form sent suddenly from heaven
That whispered to them each, " Forgive, as ye would be forgiven ; "
For hands were clasped, and trusting smiles began to beam again,
And chastened and repenting words removed the sting of pain.

They tell us poetry's a thing we cannot understand,
All dreamy and intangible, borne from an unreal land ;

Yet surely there are fireside scenes, and deeds, and words, and looks
More thrilling than romance can be, in all the startling books.
There must be poetry where love perfumes the atmosphere,
Where language is composed alone of all that can endear,
Where of unselfish sympathy the passing life is full.
Let us *live poetry*, and earth will be so beautiful!

Call to Worship.

"O come, let us worship and bow down: let us kneel before the Lord our
maker."—Psalm xcv. 6.

O COME, and let us gather,
   'Tis the holy hour of prayer;
Let united supplications
   Softly fill the scented air;
Let us wipe the clinging earth-dust
   From the heated, aching brow,
And amid the hours of labour
   Let our weary spirits bow.

We have souls that are immortal,
   And they should not grovel here,
But should rise and hold communion
   In their higher native sphere;
Let us kneel around heaven's portal,
   Till, in accents soft and sweet,
Come the whispers of Jehovah,
   Soothing all before His feet.

It is well, amid the bustle
   And the weariness and strife,
To withdraw our thoughts a moment
   From the vexing cares of life;

To ascend and join the angels
  In the lofty songs they sing,
And to chant our hallelujahs
  To the praise of Zion's King.

God has filled the world with beauty,
  Has o'ershadowed it with love,
And prepares us in His kindness
  Yet a better home above :
O ! then come, each fellow pilgrim,
  Let us worship and fall down,
Let us kneel before our Maker,
  Weaving praises for His crown.

Rest in the Ark.

"But the dove found no rest for the sole of her foot, and she returned
unto him into the ark."—Gen. viii. 9.

"No rest! no rest!" Life's rough and stormy billow
  Rises and falls amid the howling storm ;
Its changeful waters yield no resting pillow
  For weary wing and fragile fainting form.

"No rest! no rest!" So long I have been roaming,
  Uncomforted, unsatisfied, unblest,
While the wild waters all around are foaming,
  And still their sad song is—"No rest ! no rest !"

"No rest! no rest!" For ah ! I have forsaken
  The blessed ark where dwells such deep repose,
And recklessly a dangerous course have taken
  Where the dark tempest in its fury blows.

My spirit sorrows that it e'er departed
  From that sweet resting place, that tranquil shade,
Where peace and joy so solace the sad-hearted,
  And chase the shadows sin and care had made.

"No rest! no rest!" I long to be returning
  To that safe haven which once sheltered me;
My heart in its intensity is yearning
  To be thus resting, satisfied, and free.

O Thou who know'st how very dark and dreary
  Is the long passage taken thus alone,
Receive the drooping dove, all worn and weary,
  Into Thy loving arms—again Thine own!

Speak Kindly.

Speak kindly! Ah! thou knowest not
  How much of good or ill
May be within the little words
  Thou speakest lightly still—
How long within the yearning heart
  Their influence may remain,
Gilding the life with beams of joy,
  Or shading it with pain.

Speak kindly! Crushing trials come
  To every pilgrim here,
And earth, with all its tinselled show,
  Is desolate and drear;
But kindly, sympathizing words
  Bring sunshine, peace, and rest:
O! soothe the weary, aching head,
  And ease the throbbing breast.

Speak kindly! Words are registered
In God's own book in heaven;
And O! remember, not in vain
The least of them is given.
Then earn the blessing of the sad,
While life's short course ye run,
And pray that thou may'st hear at last
Thy Father's sweet " Well done!"

Tarry with us.

WHEN the night-clouds gather o'er us,
Shutting out the light of day;
When the path is dark before us,
Saviour, Thou canst see our way:
Tarry with us,
And we shall not go astray.

When life's changing scenes distress us.
Fill our quaking hearts with fear;
Care and grief and pain oppress us,
Burden the thick atmosphere:
Tarry with us,
All is well if Thou art near.

When, amid the consternation,
Breathing silent prayers we kneel
Craving help and consolation
For the woes our spirits feel,
Tarry with us,
Jesus, Thou alone canst heal.

When the foe we dread is bringing
Pain and death to those we love,
And the hands to which we're clinging
Loosen, and are stretched above,
Tarry with us,
Holiest, do not Thou remove.

When this weary life is ending,
When to *us* death draweth nigh,
Still Thy fainting ones be tending,
And we will not fear to die :
Tarry with us,
Saviour, bear us to the sky.

_____

"I sat under his shadow with great delight."

Solomon's Song, ii. 3.

I LOOKED at the past, at the joys which had fled,
At the sunshiny hours that had passed o'er my head,
At the seeming good deeds that I ever had done,
And sought there for comfort; alas! I found none.

I looked at the future, which brightly did gleam—
Tried to gather some hope from its joy-lighted dream;
But a shadowy mist passed over the whole,
Leaving nothing to fill the desires of my soul.

Then I turned from both, counting each one but dross,
And faintingly sank at the foot of the Cross;
And the Saviour came to me so loving and mild,
And pressed in His arms His dissatisfied child.

Then I buried my face in His bosom and wept,
That His easy commands I so feebly had kept;
But His soul-thrilling voice bade my sorrows all cease,
And, in accents of love, He breathed o'er me His peace.

And my spirit's deep yearnings were instantly still—
For the love of the Saviour each craving can fill;
And I only drew nearer and nearer His side,
And asked that for ever I there might abide.

And I gazed in His eye, till my heart soared above,
And was filled with deep draughts of ineffable love;
Earth's trifles all faded away from my sight,
As I sat 'neath His shadow, and found great delight.

Coming up from the Wilderness.

THE twilight shades my future way are hiding,
    Darkness will spread its pall;
How sweet to feel the Infinite abiding
    Here, where the shadows fall!

I've laid my hand in His, and He is leading—
    Whither I do not know;
But in the pastures of His love I'm feeding,
    Where living waters flow.

And though at times this life's intricate mazes
    Are very rough and long;
My spirit clings to His strong arm, and raises
    The pilgrim's holy song.

And when—the path grown very dark and dreary—
 I faint, and yearn for rest,
Sweet are the slumbers of the worn and weary,
 On the Beloved's breast.

I fear not, though the furious tempest rages,
 While He still whispers *Peace!*
For His calm voice the wildest storm assuages,
 And all its dashings cease.

Upon my brow He has "Excelsior" graven,
 And so I soon shall soar,
And leave this wilderness for His bright haven
 Where I shall love Him more.

Looking up.

"I will direct my prayer unto thee, and will look up."—Psalm v. 3.

WHEN the woes of life oppress me,
 And my heart grows faint with grief,
And there's no one near to bless me,
 Nor to give my soul relief,
I will look to Thee, my Father,
 To Thy blessed footstool cling;
For Thou lov'st the weak to gather
 'Neath Thy kindly fostering wing.

When the light of joy is beaming
 O'er the fair and brilliant way,
And the flowers of life are seeming
 As if ne'er to fade away,—

For Thy love, which knows no measure,
  And Thy smile so freely given,
Will intensify each pleasure,
  And make earth almost like heaven.

When the hills of life grow steeper,
  And the way is rough and long,
When the darkened mists grow deeper,
  And my heart becomes less strong,—
For there's none but Thee to guide me
  Through the torrent or the brake—
I will pray, "O, go beside me,
  Every step my feet may take!"

And when death its dews is wreathing
  Round the brows of those I love,
And the faded lips are breathing
  Sighs for ease and rest above;
When all skill is unavailing,
  And my woe is great indeed,
Then Thy love will be unfailing,
  And will meet my spirit's need.

When the shades of life are closing
  O'er the landscape of my life,
And I yearn to be reposing
  From its weariness and strife,
'Mid the waves of Jordan's river
  Shall my prayer ascend to Thee—
I will look to Thee for ever,
  Here and in eternity.

"Hold Thou me up, and I shall be safe."

Psalm cxix. 117.

FATHER! I cannot walk alone;
  The pathway that I tread
Is all too difficult for me,
  Unless by Thee I'm led.
But Thou art strong, and wise, and good;
  Thou know'st the way I take ;
O ! let my weakness cling to Thee ;
  Lead me, for Jesus' sake !

For I shall wander from Thy side
  When danger may be near,
And faint along the wayside rough,
  O'erwhelmed with grief and fear,
Unless Thy mighty hand, O God!
  Uphold me all the time,
And guide me every step I take
  Toward the heavenly clime.

Yes! hold me, and I shall be safe,
  And let me ever be,
Through the intricate maze of life,
  Clinging to none but Thee.
O ! keep me by Thy mighty love
  Still in the narrow way,
Until the darkness of this world
  Melts into perfect day.

"The Lord hath need of thee."

CHILD, who art dancing with careless feet
Through the pathway where pleasure and plenty meet,
There's a still small voice sweetly calling thee ;
The Friend of thy childhood has need of thee !
Not to gather one flower from thy sunny way,
But to make it fair with a brighter ray.
Thou on whose brow is the dew of youth,
Whose eye is bright with the light of truth,
He who is God of the realms above
Has need of thee with thy heart of love ;
Not to stay thy step in its buoyancy,
But to fill thy spirit with ecstacy.
Thou who art strong in thy manhood's prime,
To whom dost thou consecrate thy time ?
There's a noble mission from sorrow free ;
The God of the nations has need of thee !
Come, and the path which thy feet may press
Shall be carpeted over with happiness.
Whoever, whatever, thy life may be,
Listen—the Lord hath need of thee !
There are conquerors' crowns and seats of rest
For His servants, who only are truly blest.
Come where the soul is from sorrow free ;
Come, for our Master hath need of thee.

Light.

HARK! through the dense and misty air
There is rising slowly a startled prayer.
A piercing cry through the gathering night.
A wild entreaty—" O, give us light!"
And straining eyes through the darkness peer,
Earnestly asking if day be near.

Light! Light! For we cannot see
Things as they are and ought to be!
Dangers are round us —and O, for light
To read the directions of God aright!
His " hand-writing" is clear and wise :
O! that the darkness would leave our eyes!

Light for the rich, for they do not know
The duties that from their station grow!
Light for the scorned and trodden poor,
To help them to suffer and still endure!
Light for the nations that groaning lie
'Neath the weight of darkness and misery!

Light to live in this troublous time,
When terror gathers in every clime;
Light to die, to dispel the gloom
That curtains grimly the opening tomb;
O Thou who dwell'st where there is no night,
Hear us in heaven—O, give us light!

The Wife's Farewell.

Th' autumnal sunset dyed the western skies,
And threw a softened glory o'er the earth ;
The cooling breezes played among the brown
And yellow leaves, and woke within the woods
Wild, thrilling music-tones.

        And there was one
Whose last request had been to have her couch
Drawn to the window, that she might once more
Drink in the beauty of this lovely earth.
Her deep blue eyes were filled with tears, as oft
She turned from the sweet scene without, and laid
Her trembling fingers on her husband's head,
Or smoothed the damp locks from his burning brow,
Until he murmured, in tones of agony,
" How can I live without thee ?"

        Then she turned
Towards him, with a look of deathless love,
And, with a sweet smile resting on her lips,
Said, in a tone of melting tenderness :—

" Thou wilt not, precious one,
    For souls so linked as ours can never part ;
Death seals the eye and silences the tone,
    But cannot touch the heart.

" And, dearest, *we* have loved
    With an unchangeable—a deathless love ;
Begun on earth, to be still further proved,
    And perfected above.

"Dost thou remember well
How full of happiness our lives have been—
Dwelling together in this lovely dell,
So holy and serene—

"Where not one grief has come,
And not one sorrow thrown its darkening shade
Over the sunlight of our happy home,
Which love so sweet has made?

"Ah! thou wilt ne'er forget
The brow, the heart, that throbbed alone for thee;
The love that clings to thee in death—and yet
I struggle to be free.

"For I am going home—
Home, where the weary ones so sweetly rest;
Where thou, my best-belovèd, soon shalt come,
And lean on Jesus' breast.

"The time will not be long;
Life's shadows lengthen o'er thy shortening way;
Thou soon wilt swell the loud, triumphant song,
Where there is no decay.

"And I will ask to come
And float around thee in thy sombre hours,
When evening's shadows fill thy lonely room,
And dew rests on the flowers;

"And fan thy aching brow
With the cool, soothing airs of Paradise;
And raise the spirit that is drooping now,
To soar beyond the skies.

" Our love has been so deep,
 And I so happy in thy company,
I scarce could stay in heaven if thou didst weep—
 I'd fly to comfort thee.

" Ah! I am going now—
 Start not, my husband—only closer fold
Thy shielding arms about me—kiss my brow,
 That grows so damp and cold.

" Lay me upon thy heart;
 I long to die on that sweet resting-place;
And, dearest, smile upon me ere we part;
 I scarce can see thy face.

" Let my last dying breath
 Be gently breathed upon thy lips—for, O!
Thou art so very dear to me in death;
 Farewell, belov'd—I go.

" See, angel-forms of light
 Beckon me softly to the golden shore;
I long to go where all things are so bright,
 And I shall weep no more.

" I can hear music sweet
 From the unnumbered lyres with golden strings,
And happy ones who lie at Jesus' feet,
 And sing of holy things.

"O! earth, with all its love,
 Is nothing with this land of bliss in view;
Its ties are loosening, and I mount above,
 Detain me not. Adieu!"

The stricken husband went upon his way;
But, ere the autumn came again, he joined
His loved and lost one in that peaceful land
Where the heart's clinging cords are never riven.

"Lord, teach us to pray."

My Saviour, O my Saviour! how I long to come to Thee!
As, prostrated before Thee, I am here on bended knee;
But my tongue can find no utterance, I know not what to say,
And can only groan in spirit—teach, O teach me how to pray!

This should be the hour of freedom, of communion with the skies,
But my thoughts are all so earth-bound that they cannot, will not rise;
And my restless, panting spirit vainly struggles to be free;
It cannot make this world its home, yet cannot come to Thee.

O! if Thy hand of love would wipe this sin-stain from my brow,
Then I might raise my eyes to heaven, and see Thy face; but now
This ponderous weight of guilt will press me down to earth again.
I am saddened and disheartened, for my efforts seem in vain.

O! that heaven were but nearer, and Thyself less far away!
That from Thy throne in glory Thou wouldst teach me how to pray
But I may not expect it—Thou dost justly hide Thy face
From one who cannot love Thee, and who values not Thy grace.

Yet linger near me, Saviour; leave me not in sadness here,
For this wilderness, without Thee, is so lonely and so drear;
The tempest round is raging, and I fearful, trembling stand;
O! through the dense, dark mist, Redeemer, stretch to me Thy hand.

Then will I give to Thee this heart, for Thou wilt scorn it not,
But in the stream of Calvary cleanse it from each dark spot,
And from my spirit's soarings take this crushing weight away.
Jesus, I thank Thee : surely now Thou'rt teaching me to pray.

The Great Physician.

"Now when the sun was setting, all they that had any sick with divers diseases brought them unto him; and he laid his hands on every one of them, and healed them."—Luke iv. 40.

JUDÆA's hills were with sunset dyed,
The soft breeze stirred by the river's side,
And weary feet o'er the way-side prest;
The children slept on their mothers' breast,
And the deepening hush at the daylight's close
Brought soothing whispers of sweet repose.

But the Saviour of sinners rested not,
His labours and grief were all forgot;
He stood, with pitiful, loving eye,
Marking the groups that were drawing nigh,
For a sorrowing, suffering, sickly train
Came o'er the mountain, and vale, and plain.

The blind with his sightless orbs drew near,
The trembling leper, o'erwhelmed with fear;
The idiot came, with his wandering eye;
The deaf and dumb, with the deep-fetched sigh;
The palsied limb, and the fevered brow,
Thronged at the Healer's feet to bow.

And with loving mercy He laid His hand
On "every one" of the strange, sad band;
And the healing touches new joy awoke,
And a shout of praise on the silence broke;
For many a home was illumed with light
That had been all dark till that happy night.

O! when the shadows of evening fall,
When the inward voices to worship call,
And we come to Thee on our lowly knees,
Heal us, dear Saviour, of sin's disease;
Remove the sickness that clouds our days,
Loosen the tongues that would sing Thy praise.

The Closing Scene.

WE know not what it is to pass death's deep and awful gloom,
Nor why we all should shudder so in prospect of the tomb;
But we dread to think of agonies that are so fierce and strong,
When mysterious voices tell us they will all be ours ere long.

For O! *to die*, and leave this world with light and beauty filled;
To feel the life-blood in our veins flow sluggishly and chilled;
To know the boundings of our hearts are by death's finger crushed,
And our breath is growing quick and short, and then for ever hushed.

To be conscious that all things around grow dark and fade away,
That that dense night is coming on, and shrouding all our way;
That e'en our loved and loving ones are with the dim unknown;
To be launched in Jordan's cold, deep flood, and feel we are alone.

Alone! O no! for let us now betake ourselves to prayer,
That He who conquered Death himself may stand beside us there ;
That Jesus' arms may shield us from the mighty monster's power,
And we may closely cling to Him in that most trying hour.

And then we will not fear to die, but gladly close our eyes,
To open them 'mid brighter scenes beyond the azure skies.
We know that to a "better land" our ransomed souls will come,
And will not shrink from dying, since it is but "*going home.*"

One More in Heaven.

THE azure skies have opened, and an angel has been down,
To bring glad tidings for an heir to an immortal crown :
A chilling hand was softly laid upon the failing heart,
And, freed, the spirit fled away to act a nobler part.

What glory burst upon the sight that here had been so dim ;
How bright his eyes, while those below shed many tears for him ;
How full of joy he must have been, though earth's slight cords were
    riven ;
How glad he must have felt to think he made one more in heaven !

One more to bend with perfect love before the Saviour's feet ;
One more that still increasing throng with thankfulness to greet ;
One more to swell that thrilling song he practised oft below ;
One more in heaven to welcome us when we are called to go.

O! comfort us with thoughts like these, dear Saviour, in Thy love,
When friends have left our hearths and homes to dwell with Thee
    above ;
And let us feel that when to us Thy signal shall be given,
We only have to close our eyes—then be "one more in heaven."

The Story of the Cross.

THE snow lay thick on the mountain top,
　And covered the frozen ground,
And the leaden skies looked darkly down
　On the ice-blocks scattered round.

And a few, close wrapped in the shielding skins,
　Came pressing around the blaze,
And paused to list to the old man's tale,
　But listened with vacant gaze.

Yet the servant of God spoke earnestly
　To the sullen Greenlanders,
Seeking the language that most of all
　The spirit's emotion stirs.

He spoke of the Highest, who built the world,
　And fashioned the sea and skies,
And solemnly told His perfections o'er—
　How holy, how good, how wise.

But their hearts were cold as the snow around,
　And the dull and vacant stare
Half chilled the hope of the servant's soul,
　And checked the aspiring prayer.

But a better thought came suddenly,
　As, with smiling brow and look,
And a quick, impulsive prayer to God,
　He opened the Holy Book,

And read from the pages the simple lore
  Of the dear Redeemer's love,
And told of His sufferings here below,
  And His yearning heart above.

And his soul waxed warm with the holy theme,
  And their hearts began to melt,
And the quivering lip and the tearful eye
  Told what the spirit felt.

And they looked at the good man wistfully,
  As word after word was given ;
And the cold dull souls became filled with love,
  As they plumed their wings for heaven.

Ah ! while we are treading life's thorny way,
  'Mid the sin, and toil, and loss,
There's nothing so sweet and beautiful
  As the story of the Cross.

Let us Pray.

In the bright, unclouded freshness
  Of our joyous youthful days,
When our careless feet are bounding
  Through the earth's intricate maze ;
When fair hope a brilliant sunbeam
  Lightly o'er the future throws,
And the heart, all joy and gladness,
  Nought of coming sorrow knows—
For a guide across the desert,
  For a hand whose grasp is strong,
For a lamp to light our footsteps,
  As we journey thorns among

For a check to all temptations
  That surround our unshod feet,
For a shield, a friend, a guardian,
  Who will help all woe to meet :
For a safeguard on our way—
Brother, sister, let us pray !

In the gathered congregation,
  In the rapt, adoring crowd,
When the cries of praying hundreds
  Reach the heavens long and loud :
When from hearts, like burning incense,
  Deep and fervent prayers arise,
Each in beautiful devotion
  Pouring forth its sacrifice—
For the souls that lie in darkness,
  For the heathen and the slave,
For the weather-beaten seaman,
  For the warrior and the brave;
For the widow and the orphan,
  For the poor without a home,
For the aged and afflicted,
  For the prodigals who roam ;
For a brighter, happier day—
Brother, sister, let us pray !

When our friends are gathered round us,
  And our hearts o'erflow with joy,
Tasting earnests of the pleasures
  That will never fade or cloy ;
When life's fairest flowers are scattered
  Brightly o'er the path we tread,
And the halo and the sunbeam
  Rest upon each loved one's head—

For the dear Redeemer's blessing,
  For a share in His deep love,
For a lowly reverent feeling,
  Turned towards His throne above;
For a hope of a re-union
  In the land where partings cease;
For a foretaste of the glory,
  And the purity, and peace;
For the hastening of that day—
Brother, sister, let us pray!

In the closet, closed and secret,
  When we pant for quick relief,
When our hearts lie crushed and bleeding
  'Neath their mighty weight of grief;
When our souls for love are yearning,
  And our " summer friends" have fled,
And the flowers we fondly cherished
  Lie around us bruised and dead—
For the strength of the Almighty,
  To support our fainting soul;
For the touch of the Physician
  Whose skilled hand can make us whole;
For the spirit of the Saviour,
  Still to say, " Thy will be done;"
For the rest and consolation
  He can give each wearied one;
For His love to light our way—
Brother, sister, let us pray!

At all times and in all seasons,
  Hours of darkness and of light,
All the summer, all the winter,
  Every day, and every night;

In all joy and in all sadness,
 Whether sorrowful or gay,
Whatsoever be our feelings,
 O! 'tis beautiful to pray!
Of our cares our souls are lightened
 Soon as we draw near the throne,
When our Friend, our loving Father,
 Kindly listens to His own;
And the highest, richest blessings—
 Blessings that will ne'er grow dim,
Flow round those in rich abundance
 Who draw near and pray to Him. ·
Then for ever, day by day,
Brother, sister, let us pray!

Songs in the Night.

"Who giveth songs in the night."—Job xxxv. 10.

DARK the night-clouds gather round us,
 Grief and fear beside us stand,
Sorrow and distress have bound us,
 Pressing us on every hand.
Yet, the songs of Zion singing,
 Tranquil 'mid it all we dwell;
Every night, its blessing bringing,
 Helps the choral strain to swell.

For we know that still above us
 Is the Guardian of the night,
Who will ever cheer and love us,
 Who will bring us peace and light.

And so sweet is our communion
  'Mid the weary journeying,
So intense and close the union,
  That we cannot choose but sing.

'Tis His love inspires the chorus,
  'Tis His grace suggests the song,
'Tis His favour shining o'er us
  Makes the night seem not so long;
For each day that has departed
  Came with blessings from His hand,
Solacing the weary-hearted,
  Shedding light across the land.

O! for grace to serve Him better!
  For a heart to love Him more,
Free from sin's debasing fetter,
  Upward to His throne to soar!
Jesus! give us warmer feeling,
  O! increase our spirit's light,
Till around Thy throne we're kneeling,
  Where there will be " no more night."

The Spirit's Light.

"And it was now dark, and Jesus was not come to them."—John vi. 17.

'Tis always dark when Jesus has not come!
  Solemn and stormy is the way of life;
Gloom settles o'er the fairest hearth and home,
  And nought is seen and felt but woe and strife.

'Tis never dark where He will deign to be;
  O'er life's sad hours a joy sublime He flings;
Our weary hearts from fear and care grow free,
  While He is watching o'er our precious things.

His presence is the brightness of our day,
  His absence is the darkness of our night;
We need no sunshine but His cheering ray—
  Than His effulgent smile no other light.

When from His side our souls by sin are riven,
  Life's fairest joys are incomplete and dim;
But earth grows radiant with the light of heaven
  While we are holding intercourse with Him.

O! might we live for ever in His sight,
  And never mourn that Jesus has not come,
Till we behold Him as the only light*
  Within the precincts of our shining home!

"Let me Languish into Life."

A DEEP subduing glory softly hung
O'er the rich summer skies. The sweet perfume
Of honeysuckle, rose, and heliotrope,
Blent with the soft, pure air which gently stole
In at the open casement, and then fanned
The high, white forehead of the dying one.
The unbound locks lay carelessly upon
The snowy pillow, damp with death's cold dew.
The breath came feebly through the parted lips,

* Rev. xxi. 23.

And the blue eye, unnaturally bright,
Roamed to and fro, save sometimes, when it beamed
Unutterable tenderness upon
The trembling forms beside her.

They were there
Whose love had made her young life beautiful,
Hushing the breathings of their bleeding hearts,
And vainly yearning for the power to snatch
Their precious one from the cold, freezing arms
Of death. At length one took the wasted hand
And asked her if she knew them. For a while
She strove to dwell upon the scene around,
And give the answer love desired ; but, ere
Her quivering lips had formed the words, her soul
Flew to another subject, and a smile,
Intensely beautiful, illumed her face,
As, with a thrilling tone, she said, " *I know
That my Redeemer liveth !*"

Fainter grew
The pulse of life ; and o'er her eyes there stole
A thickening mist, darkening the well-known room.
She heard, as in a dream, a husky voice
Say, sadly, " She is going." Then she saw
Floating around her seraphs robed in light ;
And one, the fairest of them all, leaned o'er,
And loosed the " silver cord "—*and she was free !*
Up through the dazzling depths of light she rose,
Surrounded by ethereal beings, till
The gate of the Celestial City stood
Before them in its beauty. 'Twas not closed
To them ; and she, the newly-born, walked in.
The shining angels brought the blood-washed robe,

I

And threw around her.   On her brow they placed
The fadeless crown of life, and in her hands
A harp with strings of gold.   And then they led
Her on, and on, and on, o'er the vast plains
Studded with amaranthines—till she gained
The temple of the Holiest.

There she stayed;
Her spirit bathed in rapture, and drank in
Melodious music from unnumbered lyres,
And sweet, unfaltering voices.   There she saw
Myriads of beings clothed in radiant robes,
And ONE, more beautiful than all beside,
Who seemed the source of all the dazzling light.
Nearer she drew to Him, and then she saw
The wounded hand and pierced side, and knew
That it was Calvary's Sufferer!   With a cry
Of rapturous adoration, low she knelt
Before His great white throne, and cast her crown
At His dear feet.   Then, in His mighty love,
He raised and folded her in His kind arms,
And bade her welcome to her home in heaven!

When morning dawned, earth had another scene
Of agonizing woe.   A little band
Of stricken mourners stood beside the clay,
And wept that earth was darker still.

But heaven:

Ah! *there was joy in heaven!*

An Appeal to the Undecided.

"How long halt ye between two opinions?"—1 Kings xviii. 21.

THERE's a long broad path, and the sky looks fair,
And the road is smooth, and serene the air;
There's a narrow way which is often long,
And tempests gather and dangers throng.
Lingerers, choose as ye will to-day—
The pleasant path or the narrow way.

There are flattering lips and faces bold,
Deceiving spirits and hearts all cold;
There's a Friend whose every thought is love,
A guiding hand to the realms above.
Halters, to whom shall your trust be given—
Earth's fair, false friends, or the God of heaven?

There's a wreath of roses that droop and die;
There's a smile that hides the convulsive sigh;
There's a crown of life that will ne'er decay;
There are sunlight joys that fade not away.
Doubters, to which shall your spirits bow?
Which is the coronal for your brow?

The end of the long broad path is death,
In blackness and woe giving up the breath;
But the narrow way leadeth still above,
To immortal bliss and unchanging love.
Ye who are undecided, come
To that peaceful world, that eternal home.

A Sabbath Scene.

EARTH was hung o'er with an unclouded sky,
And carpeted with a green velvet sward.
Beauty—such beauty as the Infinite
Alone creates—lay everywhere around;
And it was full of low, sweet melody.
The singing birds poured their glad anthems forth,
As if they did so joy in life, and knew
Their morning song was wholly due to Him
Without whose knowledge not a sparrow falls;
The pebbly brook murmured its thrilling sounds;
And ever and anon the fragrant air
Breathed the sweet music of the Sabbath bells.
The crowded city, too, looked like repose,
For, though there many were with hardened hearts
Who would not hear the voice inviting them
To rest and happiness, yet were the marts
And warehouses, and busy haunts of man
Closed and deserted.

      But there was one house,
A holy, consecrated fane, whose doors
Opened invitingly, and whose fair aisles
Were trod with silent reverence and joy,
As one by one the worshippers came in.
The man of wealth came with his family;
And he whose hands were hard and brown with toil
Led in his children, and their mother too.
The merchant, leaving his bewildering books,
His counting-house, and stores, came gently in,
To lave his burning brow and weary heart
In that blest river whose cool streams make glad
"The city of our God." And the old man,

Longing once more to hear the Gospel news,
Leaned on the arm of his tall, stalwart son,
Who led him gently to his well-worn seat,
And sat beside him. Then a little band,
Who through the long, long days had sat and stitched,
Earning their daily bread, came wistfully
For His kind messages who loves to give
The weary rest. And she whose snow-white brow
And bounding heart knew little of the touch
Of sorrow, laid her joy-tinged dreams aside,
And came to sit before His sacred feet
Who is the Fount of Love.

      Then there stole
A deeper awe o'er the assembled crowd,
As the beloved and aged pastor came,
Bearing upon his thoughtful countenance
The traces of a hallowed interview;
For he had been with Jesus.

      Sweetly came
The words of invitation, " Let us pray ! "
And then the knee was bent, and the high brow
Laid low, and the full heart echoed the prayer—
" Give us Thy blessing, Lord of light and love ! "
O ! it was beautiful to see the rich
Kneeling beneath the lofty dome where knelt
The lowly peasant ; and upon the face
Of all to see a holy, tranquil joy,
Such as the world with all its glittering show
Could never give.

     And then, filling the place
Arose the rapturous, thrilling strain, " O come,
And let us sing unto the Lord, and let
Us make a joyful noise unto the Rock

Of our salvation." And it seemed as if
They were rehearsing for the festival
Of hallelujahs they would swell above.
And when the pastor said, with beaming eye
And trembling utterance, "In my Father's house
Are many mansions," what a thrill of joy
Passed through the aching hearts around!

                                    He told
The weary they would there find rest; the sad
That they should drink fulness of joy; the poor
That they were heirs to untold wealth; the sick
That *there* should be no pain; and the bereaved
That death ne'er enters that blest meeting place.
He told the happy that their highest joy
Was nothing when compared with the deep bliss
Of the eternal mansions.

                                    So he seemed
To have a message for them all. And O!
How many wished they were already there!
But, when he breathed the benediction o'er
The low-bowed heads—and when he bade them still
Go back into the world, and be like Him
Who lived, and loved, and laboured, but ne'er sinned—
They felt that life was earnest, and went out
Strong in the strength of the Almighty One!

Heaven.

THERE's a *home* of happy meetings,
   Meetings never more to part,
Where the sounds of joyous greetings
   Thrill through every bounding heart;

Where lost friends will find each other,
    Catch the love-lit glance again,
Clasp the hand of father, mother,
    And in perfect love remain.

There are *streams*, where pilgrims weary
    Stay and lave their dusty feet,
Grateful that the path, though dreary,
    Brought them to an end so sweet;
Where the drooping hearts recover,
    Leaning on the Saviour's breast,
While around them angels hover,
    And they all are truly blest.

There are *shrines*, where spirits glorious
    Lay the relics of their strife,
And on warriors' brows victorious
    Gleam the fadeless " crowns of life ; "
Where no trace of earth-dust lingers
    On the trophies which they bring;
And where fair untrembling fingers
    Take the palm-branch of their King.

There are *altars*.   In devotion
    Seraphs fold their radiant wings,
And the pure, with deep emotion,
    Bow, and breathe of holy things;
And, in one long strain of blessing,
    Lips that are from faltering free,
Faultless harpists, gold lyres pressing,
    Join the holy minstrelsy.

Father! when life's shadows lengthen,
    And its sunset gilds the dome,
Give us light and hope to strengthen
    Longings for our better home;

Cheer us, when our hearts are fainting,
With the music of the blest;
Show us of that world a painting:
Then, O take us to Thy rest!

The Resolve.

Thou shalt guide me with thy counsel, and afterward receive mɪ
to glory."—Psalm lxxiii. 24.

YES, Thou shalt guide me, kind and gentle Father,
Through all this desert wild;
I ask not for its brightest joys, but rather
That I may be Thy child.

I cannot go alone, unloved, untended,
Through life's untrodden way;
For oft into forbidden paths I've wended,
And still may go astray.

My future journey looks so dark and dreary,
Its hills so steep and long;
But, O! 'tis sweet, when very faint and weary,
To lean upon the Strong.

And though I cannot see a step before me,
Though clouds my pathway hide,
I fear not while Thy love is shining o'er me,
My kind, unerring Guide.

And so I close my ear to other voices,
And hearken unto Thine;
My spirit drinks Thy counsel, and rejoices,
Tasting of life divine.

Earth's storms my fragile leaning-trusts are flinging
 Far from my grasp away;
But, closely to the "Rock of Ages" clinging,
 My soul feels no dismay.

Then lead me on, dear Saviour, in Thy kindness,
 Through paths Thy feet have worn,
Unspotted by the world's deep sin and blindness,
 Unto that glorious bourne—

Where seraphs crowned with glory will receive me,
 And take me to Thy breast,
No more to disobey, forget, or grieve Thee,
 But bathe in perfect rest.

"For to me to live is Christ, and to die is Gain."

Phil. i. 21.

I AM waiting, I am waiting, and I fain would fly away,
And feel this darkness melting into pure, undying day;
Would soar at once to heaven, and there breathe my native air,
Where gathering shadows fall no more, where all is calm and fair.
To be going, to be going—ah! I long to go e'en now,
To drop this heavy weight of care for ever from my brow.
Earth is a sad and sinful place, and heaven is my home;
Why are its messengers so slow when fetching me they come?

I am weary, very weary, and I long to be at rest,
To recline these throbbing temples on the Saviour's gentle breast,
To see my Jesus, as He is, in realms of light above,
And live for ever in His smile, and drink deep draughts of love.

And the glory—ah! the glory that is waiting for me there;
How my spirit pants to reach it, and its blessedness to share—
To receive a harp of gold, a crown of pure and radiant light!
How can I linger longer in this world of sin and night?

Yet 'tis sinful, very sinful, thus impatiently to crave
What can only be my own after passing through the grave;
After waiting, watching, working till my sovereign Lord's command
Shall bear me far away from earth to that celestial land.
O my Father! O my Father! pray forgive Thy erring child,
Whose spirit, after all Thou'st done, is unsubdued and wild;
And make me quiet in Thy hands, submissive to Thy will,
Who silencest my soul's strong strife by whispering, " Be still!"

Make me anxious, make me anxious, less at once the world to leave
Than to make more like a heaven on earth the spot whereon I live;
And make more holy, and more pure, my whole deportment here,
So that upon my brow may shine the Saviour's image clear;
Then how happy, O! how happy, when the call at last is given,
Shall I be to find that scarcely I a stranger am to heaven;
That my spirit has been purified as that fair light-robed throng,
And my lips have here been sweetly trained to echo heaven's own
    song!

"And he was not, for God took him."

How peacefully the Christian falls asleep!
    How tranquilly he sinks to his repose!
Closing the eyes that never more shall weep,
    Easing the heart that aches with no more woes,
Breathing his life away on that kind breast
Where the world-weary lie in perfect rest!

God takes him! One by one the clinging ties
 That bind his heart to earth are gently riven,
And o'er his spirit brighter beams arise,
 While fond anticipations turn to heaven;
And, as his eyes wax dim, the world appears
Enfolded in a shroud of grief and tears.

The mortal frame grows weaker day by day;
 The wasting hands beside him strengthless fall,
The shortening breath dies silently away,
 And soft, mysterious voices sweetly call:
Almighty arms enfold, and bear him on
Ere mourning friends can whisper, "He is gone."

On through the depths of heaven's eternal light,
 Where hallejujahs fill the fragrant air—
Where saints and angels welcome with delight,
 And hearts are happy amidst scenes so fair—
Where neither age, nor weariness, nor pain can come:
O, it were sweet to be, like them, *at home!*

The Christian's Home.

"He that dwelleth in the secret place of the Most High shall abide
under the shadow of the Almighty."—Psalm xci. 1.

O! BUT to be within that sacred dwelling,
 O! but to have that shadow for our home,
While life's rough billows are around us swelling,
 While o'er its shifting sands we trembling roam!

Thrice happy all who, in that stronghold hiding,
 Are safe from earthly tempests and alarms,
'Mid calm, unruffled peacefulness abiding,
 Encircled in those everlasting arms!

There's an Almighty Friend who loveth ever,
  A heart of tenderness that ne'er grows cold,
A leaning-trust that no rude change can sever,
  A clasping hand that will not loose its hold!

And *there* are streams of life for all the thirsting,
  Fingers to guide all those who would be led,
Sweet healing for the spirits that are bursting,
  Soft resting-places for the aching head!

O pitiful All-loving, we are yearning
  To rest beneath the shadow of Thy wing!
O! help the faltering few that are returning;
  Unto that " secret place " our spirits bring!

Labour and Love.

LABOUR! there are voices calling
  Ever to life's battle-field!
Rise! and join the lasting conflict
  With a will that cannot yield.

Linger not 'mid idle pleasures,
  Labour! there's enough to do;
Be thy watchword " Work and conquer!
  God's own might shall help thee through.

Men are rushing to perdition;
  Stay, O, stay their hasty feet:
Some are 'neath life's fever fainting;
  Lead to waters cool and sweet.

Some in ignorance are dwelling ;
   Point them to pure learning's fount :
Some 'mid scenes of vice are grovelling
   Urge them toward God's holy mount.

Up and work ! but O, forget not
   All is useless without love ;
Have a heart that sympathizes—
   Soul akin to God above.

Love with love uncheck'd and boundless—
   Ever flowing, ever free,
Faithful, cherishing, forgiving,
   If thou canst, as God loves thee.

Love and labour ! Christian brother,
   Live for God ! Redeem the time ;
Onward ! higher ! faint not, rest not,
   Till thou'st gained yon far-off clime.

Abide with us.

FATHER, abide with us ! The storm-clouds gather
   In gloomy vengeance o'er the sinking head.
Go with us through our pilgrimage, dear Father ;
   Cheer with Thy smile the thorny paths we tread.

Shepherd, abide with us ! Our souls are thirsting
   For life's pure waters that around Thee flow ;
Pity the spirits that with woe are bursting ;
   O ! lead us where the heavenly pastures grow.

Saviour, abide with us! We have been clinging
  To fragile reeds that droop and pass away;
But now our souls, their clasping tendrils flinging
  Around Thy strength, ask Thee to be their stay.

Jesus, abide with us! Our hearts are weary,
  And those who blessed us with their love are gone;
Thou'rt always kind to the distressed and dreary—
  Love us, O Jesus! as we journey on.

Guardian, abide with us! Earth's ties are breaking,
  And the chill desert winds have o'er us blown;
Yet we will weep not o'er the world's forsaking,
  If it will cause us to be Thine alone.

Master, abide with us! O, be Thou ever
  Along life's pathway, in Thy mercy, nigh:
Let nothing force our hearts from Thee to sever;
  Help us to live—help us at last to die!

Phases of Life.

THIS life of ours is very BEAUTIFUL:
  Fresh, fragrant flow'rets spring along its way,
Blushing assent while we their beauties cull;
  Its sky is radiant with the sun-lit ray;
And love and smiles wait on the dutiful—
  All have a share. O! life is *beautiful.*

And life is PRECIOUS—it has links of gold,
  Binding us ever with their magic might;
And it has wealth that never can be told,
  Lodged within noble hearts that love the right
And tireless strivings in the cause of good,
And strong affections for the brotherhood.

Life too is EARNEST—there are noble deeds
  To be impressed upon its passing hour;
Balm to be poured into the heart that bleeds,
  And given to the nerveless arm more power;
"Excelsior" to be graven on the brow,
And on the hand that is to labour—"Now!"

And life is SOLEMN—for it ends so soon:
  All that we love the best will fade away;
But written in the blazing light of noon,
  There is a promise of a holier day,
When life will be immortal, and the soul
Dwell where the everlasting ages roll.

Then life should be SUBLIME—O, for the art
  To clothe it in its true sublimity!
The unflinching courage—the aspiring heart—
  The lofty purpose—and the single eye!
Author of life! Thy own high lessons give,
And teach, O, ever teach us how to live.

Pictures of Life.

MORN in the City! Busy London bridge
Was not yet trodden by the restless feet
Of its vast multitudes. The faint, grey dawn
Rested on quiet homes and sleeping eyes,
And weary toiling ones, to whom the light
Comes all too soon for aching limbs and heart.
Yet there were some astir. Two little boys,
Whose fresh and rosy cheeks and rustic garb
Bespoke them from the country, came and stood
In one of the recesses. In their hands
Were cages, prisoning some fluttering birds.
The stern oppressor Poverty had taught

Their young hearts some sad lessons, and they come
On this grey morning many weary miles
Hoping to sell the songsters, and obtain
Bread for themselves and parents; to take back
Joy to their sad and humble home. They talked
Cheeringly to each other, and their thoughts
Were busy speculating on success,
Like older venturers.

            They did not see,   ·
Until he stood before them, a tall man,
Dark-browed and stately in his mien, looking
Intently on the prisoned birds. There was
A something in his aspect which o'erawed
The boys, and half afraid, they slank away
As conscious of wrong-doing. In his hand
He held a worn valise ; a wide, dark cloak   ·
Mantled his stalwart form ; and he appeared
Weary and travel-stained. His lofty brow
Was knit as if by suffering, and his eye
And lip told to the gazer their own tale
Of calm endurance.

            Yet his powerful frame
Shook slightly as he asked, in broken tones
And foreign accent, " Here, my little boys,
How much for one of these ?"

               And then the boys
Summoned their courage and went near to him.
" A shilling, sir." He smiled, and from his purse
Drew forth the coin, and eagerly his hand
Received the trembling bird. The country lads
Looked wonderingly to see what he would do.

With gentle, tender touch his fingers passed
Over the ruffled feathers, then he pressed

His lips a moment to the soft round head,
And loosed his hand, and with a bounding joy
The bird careered above his head, and flew
In its glad liberty away!   The man
Stood watching, with emotion in his face,
Long as his eye could follow.   Then he turned
And bought another of the staring boys,
And sent it forth into the free, glad air;
And so, till *all* were gone !

                       And then with joy,
A strange, deep joy, upon his countenance,
He turned to go away.   But as he met
The astonished gaze of one who watched him there,
He stared a moment, while the warm blood rushed
Swift to his forehead, and revealed the tide
Of feeling at his heart.   He said, "*I have*
Just been released from a dark dungeon's walls,
And I can feel for prisoners !"

     *   *   *   *   *   **

                       A room
Within a lordly mansion.   The bright fire
Sent forth its ruddy glow.   The soft lamps lit
Most beautifully the lofty pictured walls,
And marble statuettes, and costly gems.
Fragrant exotics scented the warm air,
And all around in its rare beauty told
Of wealth, and tastes refined.

                   A lady sat
In careless elegance beside the blaze,
Reading a book.   And o'er her face there stole
A look of interest, as if the words
Had in them power to move that beautiful
And noble one.

K

All silently the door
Swung back upon its hinges, and a child
Of fairy loveliness came in, whispering
With voice as sweet as silvery lute, "Mamma."
The lady did not speak, nor even raise
Her eyes, but laid her fingers 'mid the curls—
The light-brown curls that lay around the neck
Of the fair little one, as if the touch
Brought quite enough of joy. The graceful head
Nestled against her robe, and looking up
She watched those kindling eyes, as rapidly
They passed from line to line ; and not a sound
Disturbed the silence. When the chapter's end
Was gained, and the rich book was laid aside,
The lady folded the child to her with
A mother's tenderness, and asked, "And now,
What is it, Lily, darling ?"

The bright eyes
Were dreamy for a moment, and the brow
Grew thoughtful ; then, with low, soft utterance,
"I've heard a pretty story, dear mamma,
About the Saviour ; how some mothers brought
Their children to Him once, and Jesus' friends,
Who knew not *all* about Him, said that He
Could not attend to little ones, and bade
Them go away. *But Jesus said,* 'O, let
The children come !' And then He smiled, and laid
His hands upon their heads, and blessed them, so
That they were always happy ! And, mamma,
I want to see the Saviour, and be blest—
Take me to Jesus, please !"

A thrill of pain
Shot through the heart to which the child was pressed.

The mother had been passing tender : all
Her love could do to brighten the young life
Of this, her only child, had been well done ;
But *she* knew not the Saviour, so her lips
Had spoken not of Him ; and this request,
Uttered so earnestly, awoke a wish
That she were not a stranger to the Lord.
But soon she stayed the yearning heart, and said,
" I cannot lead you to Him as they did,
But we will pray that He may bless you still."
There was a silent prayer, and then the words
Spoken by her, and echoed by her child,
Went as an evening sacrifice to Him—
The Great Eternal.   And the choirs of heaven
Had joyous music, for the blessing came
Both for the mother and the child, and they
Were sealed for heaven.

      *   *   *   *   *   *

                     There was a scene of woe
And dread despair !   Upon a bed there lay
A form that had been very beautiful ;
Nay, even now the features were all young
And fair and delicately formed.
But every limb writhed in intensest pain ;
The brow was knit in anguish, and the eye
Glared with a wild, unnatural light, and spoke
Such tales of suffering as made the spirit shrink.
Disease had stricken that ill-fated girl,
And all attempts to soothe the racking **pain**
Were useless.   So, her loving friends stood by,
Helpless, except to weep.   O, it was sad
To hear the shrieks that woke the startled air,
And see the little form in its agony
Of pain.

But 'twas the spirit's fever that
Awoke the mournful wail. She knew, too late,
That the fair morning of her youth had passed
In idle playfulness. Life had not been
The earnest hallowed thing God meant it should.
She had not sought in happy days of health
His love and friendship, who alone can be
The great Physician and the able Friend.

There came the night
Of darkness to her spirit, and she cried
For mercy; but despair alone replied.
At length drew near, with calm, pale brow, and eyes
Filled with the tears of sympathy, and prayer
In his full heart, a servant sent from God.
He knelt, and 'mid her shrieks he spoke the words
Of life and peace! Long days and nights he stayed,
As would his Master, wearying not, though yet
No sunshine gladdened him. And the wild heart
Still heaved with its deep anguish.

Then he told
How Christ had calmed the sea, healed the possessed,
And loved the worst of sinners. And his prayers
Arose to heaven's high portal, and at length
The tarrying blessing came! Peace, blessed peace,
Fell on the troubled spirit, and, with trust
In the Redeemer's merit, soon she died.

But had the young and gay seen *her*, methinks
They would not leave the " one thing needful" till
Life's evening hour came on !

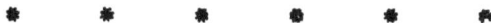

*   *   *   *   *   *

Life and its pictures! Some are dressed in hues
Of sombre aspect! Some are bright and fair,
With joy's sweet sunshine! But we all can tell
That the great Artist doeth all things well.

    *   *   *   *   *   *

The sun is setting in the distant west,
The skies are bathed as if in liquid gold,
As through the tree-tops comes a whispered strain
Of softened music-tones ; and stealing, too,
Upon the trembling air, the murmurings
Of flowing streamlets, or the sighing sea,
Blend with soft human voices.

                    Strange it is
What influence the glorious sunset has
Upon our spirits. At the morning's dawn,
Or 'neath the noontide beam, we mix among
The busy scenes of life, and murmur not;
Nay, feel that 'tis a happiness to live
And labour with our fellows. But at eve,
Though the same scenes surround us, how there comes
Stealing across our souls a yearning thought,
That makes us long to shut earth out, and bring
Heaven only in! Ah! it is then we pine
For intercourse with those, the shining ones,
Who long have breathed the holy atmosphere
Of the bright spirit-land ! We are athirst
For something deeper, holier than earth,
Although its loves and friendships are so dear.
Surely these hearts of ours are made more pure
By the soft twilight hours, and thus we learn
To love it so!

          And yet there is a kind
Of sadness in its beauty ; for we know

The day, with all its happiness, has passed
Away for ever. O'er our onward path
Its sun no more may shine, its golden hours
No more bring opportunities to speak
The kindly'word, perform the God-like deed.
"Passing away" must aye be said. But ah!
There are far sadder sunsets than the close
Of day.

  * * * * * *

   There sat a pale and wasted girl
Within a darkened room. Her classic head
Had silver threads amid the raven hair,
Though youth had not yet passed. Her marble brow
Bore marks of lofty and impassioned thought.
She had bent all her intellect to win
The meed of fame; whole days and nights
She toiled unweariedly with rapid pen
Or glowing pencil; and there came at last
A slight reward for all her care. Men praised
The eloquent heart-thoughts, that wondrously
Had power to thrill their spirits; and they called
Her "gifted," and spoke flatteringly about
Her "hallowed mission here." And so she stayed
And basked herself awhile in the bright sun,
And thought that it would always shine. But then
It quickly set, and in its place there came
The withering simoom of calumny;
And those she loved the best looked coldly on
And half believed the slander. And they tore
The wreath of laurels from her throbbing head,
And bound it with the piercing thorns of hate
And harsh suspicion, and her life henceforth
Was nought but sunless night.

  * * * * * *

There oft was seen
Walking the thronged and busy thoroughfares
Of the great city, one who looked as if
Life were all sun to him.   And when his friends
Said, " 'Tis a pleasant day," he felt the words
Had a far deeper meaning, and his heart
Would answer, " Yes, it is to me; the sun
Of bright prosperity shines round my path."
His sun was wealth; and very soon it had
A setting time.   For sudden changes came :
His riches melted from his grasp away,
And eventide of dark adversity
Came on.

      *   *   *   *   *   *

A young wife sits behind the flowers
That, with their rich, rare beauty and perfume,
Embower the open window.   The blue eyes,
Whose very depths reflect the loving heart's
Deep gladness, ever and anon look down
The half-deserted walk, and try to catch
The first short glimpse of him she loves—
How well!   She looks, too, round the pleasant room;
So many tokens of his love are there !
And as her heart recalls the words, the looks,
That were far dearer than the gifts themselves,
No wonder she exclaims, with trembling lips,
" What shall I render to the Lord for all ?
Truly, indeed, the lines have fallen to me
In pleasant places ! "

Brighter grew those eyes,
And the full lips were wreathed with smiles; for ah !
Her ear had caught the well-known sound—the step
That had such power to stir the gushing heart.

O ! there was far more welcome in that glance
Than words could frame ! Love's language would indeed
Be poor and weak and incomplete, were they
Its only messengers !

But see ! what means
That look so full of weariness and pain,
That e'en her smile can cheer not ? It is caused
By heat, perhaps, or over-weariness ;
And so he lies upon the couch, and she
Kneels close beside him, whispering low words
Of tenderness, and passing her soft hand
Lingeringly, gently o'er his heated brow,
With love's own thrilling touch.   It fills his heart
Full to o'erflowing with a grateful joy,
But cannot move the pain.   And so they call
The old physician ; and his silvery head
Is sadly shaken, for he feels his skill
Can never cool alone that heated brain.
And through the long, long days, and longer nights,
That fragile form watches beside the bed,
Tending his every wish, though but expressed
By look : her only food and rest, to stoop
And press her pallid lips upon that hand
So clammy, but so dear ! And who has power
To tell her that her young life's glorious sun
Is setting ? None, until that princely form
Lies marble-like before her, and she feels
Dense darkness all around !

    ✻   ✻   ✻   ✻   ✻   ●

Ah ! thus it is
The sunsets close about us ! Happy they
Who joy to bask beneath the glorious rays
Of Christ, the Sun of Righteousness ! No shades

Of evening dim His radiant smile; and those
Who once have welcomed Him upon life's way
Need fear no darkness. May *our* yearning hearts
Be ever lighted by His mighty love!

My Mission Here.

"WHAT is it?" asked a youth on whom the light of genius shone;
Who had a form of strength and health and vigour for his own;
Who had a power to move and guide the intellects of men,
A mighty influence o'er all who came within his ken:
"Work," was the answer, "with thy might; thy God requires of thee
That all thy powers at His command shall ever ready be."

"What is it?" asked a fragile girl; and o'er her eyes there stole
A thickening mist that seemed to shut the light out from her soul;
And all her life was marked by hours of agonizing pain,
And none was near to soothe and cheer, and bring the smile again;
"To suffer," was the answer, and she calmly took the cup,
And from a chastening Father's hand drank all its bitters up.

"What is it?" asked another, and he seemed to have a life
Of waiting for the answer. His was not the battle's strife;
He was not called to labour, nor to suffer, as are some;
Calmly and tranquilly his years would pass away or come.
He only had to *live* and meet the *little* ills of time—
With patience and contentment try to make *his* life sublime.

"My mission?" 'tis to do whate'er my heavenly Father sends,
To fulfil the present duty with the present strength He lends.
It may not be just what I wish, but then, since He knows best,
O! let me strive to do His will, and leave with Him the rest;
Assured that if He gives a life of labour or of pain,
So it be sanctified by Him, I cannot live in vain.

"Who is on the Lord's Side?"

Exodus xxxii. 26.

HAPPY child, with the cloudless brow
And sorrowless spirit—say, art THOU?
Wilt thou come with thy wreath of budding flowers,
And give to the Highest the sunny hours?
More beautiful still will thy childhood be
If thou bring'st it to Him on bended knee.

Art THOU, young man in thy healthful prime?
Wilt yield to thy God the fresh morning-time?
Wilt thou come ere the flashing eye grow dim,
Wilt bring thy talents and strength to Him?
Come! and a valiant soldier be,
For the Lord hath need of such as thee.

Mother, art THOU, with thy deathless love,
Stamped with the impress from above?
Hast thou thyself to the Holiest given?
Dost thou press on in the way to heaven?
Come! and thy priceless treasures bring
In their youth and beauty to Zion's King!

Art THOU, O man of maturer years,
With firm step treading this vale of tears?
Say, wilt thou bring the thought refined,
The unflinching arm, the unbending mind—
The glory and strength of thy manhood's pride?
O, come and enlist on Jehovah's side!

And way-worn pilgrim! say, art THOU,
With thy faltering step and thy furrowed brow?
Thy feet are trembling by Jordan's wave,
Thou art not far from the opening grave;
O tottering aged one, decide,
And join at once the Almighty's side.

O come! there is work for you all to do,
And the Captain's strength shall bear you through.
Take then the helmet, the shield, the sword;
Pass on to the banners of Christ our Lord.
Look up, for immortal crowns are there!
Flock round the standard, and "*win and wear.*"

Holy Living and Dying.

"Whether we live or die, we are the Lord's."—Rom. xiv. 8.

O! TO adopt this language is to make our life sublime,
To fling a sacred halo round the sin-stained things of time;
To make earth beautiful and pure, with Heaven's own rapture fraught,
And holiness to stamp on word, on action, and on thought.

And 'tis to clothe with radiant garb the messenger of death,
To throw a beauty o'er the scene when yielding up the breath;
To exult that when earth's cherished joys grow shadowy and dim,
The soul shall bask in quenchless light, and live for aye with Him.

One breathed them as, in manhood, on a bed of pain he lay,
Intently listening for the voice to call or bid him stay;
He lived—and Jesus' image was so stamped on heart and brow,
His holy life led many at the Saviour's feet to bow.

Another, with the dew of youth, whispered, "I am the Lord's,"
While yet around her heart were thrown life's tender silken cords;
She died—in His kind arms the Saviour bore away His own,
And, clothed with immortality, she lives before His throne.

Rests there an eye upon these lines that has not turned to heaven?
Throbs there a heart that has not yet its all to Jesus given?
Go consecrate thyself to Him, and say, "Lord, I am thine;"
And o'er thy life, and at thy death, a fadeless sun shall shine.

A Crown for the Faithful.

"Be thou faithful unto death, and I will give thee a crown of life."—Rev. ii. 10.

How oft come floating o'er me dreams of that "better land,"
Faint echoes of sweet music from that bright immortal band,
Soft murmurings of still waters, thrones of pure and dazzling white,
And radiant of glory, too, so beautiful and bright—
Of belovèd ones now joining with that fair and glorious throng,
And well-remembered voices that mingle with this song.

And I wish, O, how I wish, I could lay me down and die,
So that my unimprisoned soul might spread her wings and fly;
Nor rest until she find a home within that happy place,
And help to swell the praise of Him who saves us by His grace.
But, ah, amid those rapturous songs I heard the word "Prepare!"
Not yet the golden crown is thine; the cross thou still must bear!

But I am faint and weary. Is there very much to do—
Many trials to encounter as my journey I pursue—
Much self-denying labour, many thorns strewn o'er the way,
Many storms to overshadow the brightness of my day?
Is it wrong to wish to go at once, and stay no longer here,
Where the past is full of sadness, and the future looks so drear?

O, yes! how can I shrink from my burdens or my rod,
When so many more, and heavier, were borne by Christ my God?
When He for our salvation, all my errors to atone,
Lone and dreary, faint and weary, trod the winepress all alone?
Despised, forsaken by His friends, yet He was faithful still,
His steadfast soul unshrinking to do His Father's will.

And shall I, for whom He did all this, e'er falter as I go,—
Prove faithless to my faithful friend—forsake my God? O, no!
But watch and pray with earnestness, and strive to enter heaven,
Thinking ever that the crown to the conqu'ring one is given;
And may I feel at last, when resigning up my breath,
That the coronal is mine, and I've been " FAITHFUL UNTO DEATH."

The Heart's Response to the Saviour.

" Come unto me, all ye that labour and are heavy laden, and I will
give you rest." —Matt. xi. 28.

Saviour, we long for rest! for we have been
    Constantly toiling through the long, hot day,
And now have grown quite weary of each scene,
    And faint beneath the blinding, scorching ray;
We heard Thy invitation, and would be
With those who come and seek for rest in Thee.

Saviour, what is Thy rest? Is it to lie
    Securely folded in Thy shielding arms,
And, like a child, to slumber tranquilly,
    Fearless of earth, and all its dire alarms;
In verdant pastures by still waters laid,
And rest in perfect peace beneath Thy shade?

Saviour, give us Thy rest! O let us now
  Be overshadowed by Thy sheltering wing;
Place Thy kind hand upon our burning brow,
  And Thy deep peace around our spirits fling:
And lay Thy wearied ones upon Thy breast—
Thou dear Redeemer, give us *perfect* rest.

The Unseen Presence.

"My presence shall go with thee, and I will give thee rest."—
Exodus xxxiii. 14.

THERE are sweet impulses that float unbidden
  About the Christian's brow;
There are deep joys with sources that are hidden
  From his dim eyesight now.

He hears soft music, as of water gushing,
  Which murmurs words of love;
He feels it the wild waves of passion hushing,
  And raising him above.

His brow is soothed amidst its painful throbbing
  By hands that are unseen;
His heart is cured of all its grief and sobbing,
  And rests in joy serene.

He walks through dangers, but around him ever
  Are everlasting arms,
From whose strong grasp no power of earth can sever,
  With all its wild alarms.

He knowsnot whence it comes—this presence holy—
 But feels that it is near,
To bless, and guard, and influence him wholly,
 And life's dark hours to cheer.

And yet sometimes there is a sacred feeling
 That 'tis his Father's breast
On which he leans, and finds such blessed healing,
 Such calm, unruffled rest.

And the remembrance of these words floats o'er him,
 This promise firm and true ;
And the fulfilment of it is before him—
 The *rest* and *presence* too.

So he with confidence his way is pressing;
 For deep, unshadowed love
Allures him onward to the land of blessing—
 His own bright home above.

The Language of the Eye.

"And the Lord turned, and looked upon Peter. . . And Peter went out
and wept bitterly."—Luke xxii. 61, 62.

Ah! there's a magic power in looks that baffles all control,
To trouble the deep waters of the least impulsive soul!
Who has not wept in bitterness o'er the remembered look
Of scorn, reproach, or hatred, that from life its sunshine took ?

How much of yearning tenderness one hasty glance may tell !
What passion-throbbings for the lost—the loved, perchance too well !
One look with memories of the past the aching heart may fill,
Or with a sickening despair the shrinking spirit thrill !

No wonder Peter wept, for to the language of that eye,
So sorrowful, so tender, tears must be the best reply!
Reproach, but all forgiving love, did that one look contain;
What heart so hardened in its sin but must have throbbed with pain?

But, holy Saviour, O, how oft do we deny Thee thus!
And do those eyes look ever down so pityingly on us!
Lord, let us meet that tender glance, and, Peter-like, will we
Weep that we could have been so base to such a friend as Thee.

"Return unto thy Rest, O my Soul."

Psalm cxvi. 7.

RETURN; the night is dark and drear,
　And thou art sad and lone;
The weariness of grief cries out
　In deep and mournful tone;
Thou hast no resting-place, my soul,
　Like that which thou hast left;
Return, return. ere life itself
　Is of all joy bereft.

Return; the aching void within
　Can never *here* be filled:
Return; the spirit's hunger-cry
　Can never *here* be stilled:
Thou'rt like a dove on billows' crest,
　With weary, way-worn wing;
O, flee unto thy home and ark,
　Thou restless, yearning thing.

Return unto thy rest, my soul;
  There's welcome for thee there;
No tempest's moan, no sorrow's cry,
  There rends the startled air:
Then shalt thou cling in holy peace
  To Jesus' loving breast;
O, weary, way-worn, suffering soul,
  Return unto thy rest.

The Universal Friend.

" I have compassion on the multitude."—Matt. xv. 32.

THREE days with Jesus in the wilderness
The multitude had been. Yet no complaint
Came from the parched and hungry lips that drank
The Saviour's words. It was not needed there:
His loving eye noted the paling cheek;
And the large, mighty heart swelled with its love
For the wan sufferers. Said He, " I have
Compassion on the multitude!" He blessed
With His own hands the bread, and as they ate
Looked on them yearningly.

                    Long years have passed,
But still there is a multitude on whom
The Saviour has compassion! Other eyes
Pass haughtily their crowded den; they spurn
The wretched, hungry outcasts, as they long
For bread, and light, and blessed purity;
For man's proud heart sometimes forgets to be
Compassionate! But there are holy eyes
Upon them as they crouch: the dazzling crowns
And seraphs' wings may not draw off *that* gaze.

L

And now—as when on earth—the blessed words
Fall gently from the Saviour's lips—" I have
Compassion on the multitude!"

O! ye
Who are His own disciples, tell them so.
Go to them, *for His sake*, and bid them hope;
Seek 'mid their desolation, and impart
Joy to the wretched in your Master's words;
For He will feed them, and a better time
Shall dawn upon their darkness.

———

The Heavenly Storehouse.

" 'Tis sweet, as year by year we lose
Friends out of sight, by faith to muse
How grows in Paradise our store."

YES, there our store is growing! One by one
The links in love's fond chain are broken *here;*
But in that heavenly home the vacant seats
Are quickly filling! This drear world may be
More drear and desolate, as sink the lamps
Of sweet affection; but they brightly shine,
As did the star of Bethlehem, and guide
Our wavering feet where they and Jesus are!
" Our store in Paradise!" How the faint heart,
Weary and weak below, loves to recount
The swelling numbers! They are there whose lips
Have pressed our brow ere it had learned to ache
Beneath the world's great burden. Surely *all*
Have some fond treasure there! A mother's love
In all its deathlessness—a sister's love

In its deep tenderness—a manly form
Whose strong arm cleared the rugged, thorny way,
And made the passage beautiful ; all these,
And more, are safely landed. They have learned
The song of the redeemed—have swept their lyres,
And cast their crowns, and gazed upon the face
Of the triumphant Saviour! Ah! our friends
Are far beyond us in the heavenly lore!
But *we* are passing on! Across our path
The shadows lengthen; in the gloaming west
Our sun is setting; and a peaceful calm
Steals o'er our spirits.   Loved ones, can it be
We shall rejoin you soon ?

                    Father Divine,
Let us not fear when night enwraps us close ;
But, 'mid the darkness, guide us to those shores
Where dwell our friends in Paradise !

————

Anywhere with Jesus.

ANYWHERE with Jesus, says the Christian heart;
Let Him take me where He will, so we do not part :
Always sitting at His feet, there's no cause for fears ;
Anywhere with Jesus in the vale of tears.

Anywhere with Jesus, though He leadeth me
Where the paths are rough and long, where the dangers be !
Though He taketh from me all I love below,
Anywhere with Jesus I will gladly go.

Anywhere with Jesus in the summer's heat;
Anywhere with Jesus through the winter's sleet,
Anywhere with Jesus while the bright sun shines;
Anywhere with Jesus when the day declines.

Anywhere with Jesus, though He please to bring
Into trial's fiercest fire—into suffering :
Should He bid me work or wait, or only *bear* for Him,
Anywhere with Jesus still shall be my hymn.

Anywhere with Jesus, though it be the tomb,
With its frighting terrors, with its dreaded gloom;
Though it be the weariness of a long-drawn life,
Fainting with the constant toil, drooping in the strife.

Anywhere with Jesus, for it cannot be
Dreary, dark, or desolate where He is with me.
He will love me always—every need supply;
Anywhere with Jesus, should I live or die.

The Hope that Maketh not Ashamed.

Is it hope for *love ?*   For a wealth of friends ?
For the joy that to life its beauty lends ?
For the precious ties of the hearth and home ?
For the heart's bright sunshine where'er we roam ?
Ah, no ; for the spirit may lose its tone,
And a change pass over our loved—our own ;
And the empty heart o'er its wreck may sigh
That the hope of love can fade and die.

Is it hope for *fame?* For the laurel wreath,
And conscious pride in the heart beneath ?
For a lofty step and a noble name ?
Is this shameless hope a hope for fame ?
O, the world's applause is but empty air,
And the flatterer kneels when all else is fair ;
But the dark, dark night and beclouded day
Will drive from the path fame's light away.

Is it hope for *riches?* For wealth untold ?
For the miser's hoard ? For the precious gold ?
For a life amid ease and luxury,
With poverty's shadow ne'er coming nigh ?
O, no; for this hope is a broken reed,
It will fail the heart in its deepest need ;
And the groaning spirit will sink with woe
When such earthly props from the weak grasp go !

But the hope of *the Gospel* is better far
Than the highest hopes of worldlings are ;
It will fail us not through the march of time ;
It will cheer us yet in the changeless clime.
'Tis the hope of a true and a deathless love ;
'Tis the hope of a cloudless home above ;
'Tis the hope that a fadeless crown be given ;
'Tis a hope from God, and the hope for heaven.

The Christian's Lot.

THE Christian's lot may not be high or great,
  His earthly friends may all be poor or low ;
Yet guarding angels ever round him wait,
  And with their wings ward off the fearful foe.

And, folded in the everlasting arms,
 His inward soul is filled with deathless peace;
Religion cheers him with its heavenly charms,
 And in his heart the world's allurements cease.

O ! it is well to be a Christian here ;
 What must it be within that world above,
Where sorrow will for ever disappear
 And nought remain but endless joy and love !

"We shall be changed."

1 Cor. xv. 52.

" *We shall be changed !* O, deep, mysterious story,
 Too great for finite minds to comprehend!
We shall be changed from grace to perfect glory
 When this frail mortal life of ours shall end.

"We shall be changed!" God's mandate will be spoken,
 T' arouse with power Divine the slumbering clay;·
And earth's remaining ties shall all be broken,
 And the freed spirit gladly soar away.

"We shall be changed!" For then no more corruption,
 By eyes that gaze on Jesus, shall be seen;
And we shall worship without interruption,
 No "heaven of brass," no "parting veil" between!

"We shall be changed!" From the unshackled spirit
 The film of ignorance and sin shall fall;
And the light heart no longer will inherit
 The cares and griefs which kept it here in thrall.

" We shall be changed !"   O, when the call is given,
May we be ready—waiting to obey !
May we be changed from earthly life to heaven—
From sin to holiness, from night to day !

Be Patient.

BE patient, Christian ! Jesus teaches thee
  This lesson, oft so difficult to learn;
Check for His sake impetuosity,
  And for "the mind of Jesus" strive and yearn.
O, wild and restless, with thy anxious care,
Press to the Saviour's side ; and rest thee there.

Be patient, Christian ! Bear as Jesus bore
  With ignorance and sin on every side ;
Work as He worked, until, His pure life o'er,
  Working for thee, unmurmuringly He died.
And though there be no visible success,
Be patient still, for He at last *will* bless.

Be patient, Christian, under trials here ;
  'Mid slighted love, and wrong unmerited,
Submissive wait, and every grief severe
  Shall be, through God, a blessing on thy head.
Start not ! for He, through all the raging storm,
Will shelter in His arms thy shrinking form.

Be patient, Christian, though the hand of death
  Shall sweep away thy loving, faithful few ;
Stay the rebellious thought, the impatient breath
  Thy blinding tears hide Jesus' love from view.
Trust, and look up ! Behold how tenderly
The "Man of Sorrows" looketh down on thee.

Be patient, Christian, while thy sufferings last;
　Endure " a little while " the pain and smart;
Wish not too eagerly that all were past,
　And thou reposing weary head and heart.
Wait till thy Father calls, His time is best :
Be patient, Christian, He will give thee rest.

" Yet there is Room."

Luke xiv. 22.

SINNER ! Jesus passeth by,
Kind compassion in His eye ;
Lovingly He looks on thee.
Wouldst thou ever happy be,
Hear Him sweetly whisper, " Come,
In my arms there is yet room."

Art thou guilty ?　Bearest thou
Sin's dark stain upon thy brow,
Sinking with the weight of guilt ?
'Twas for thee His blood was spilt,
And the Saviour's voice says, " Come,
In the fountain there is room."

Seest thou the pilgrim band
Travelling to Immanuel's land ?
Join them, they are truly blest ;
Join them, and thou shalt have rest.
They God's children are—then come,
In His churches there is room.

Ah ! and there is room in heaven;
Golden harps will there be given;
Waving palms of victory,
Which the Saviour won for thee.
Then no longer from Him roam;
Come at once to Jesus, come!

"I will draw all Men unto Me."

John xii. 32.

THOU drawest us, O Saviour, with Thine everlasting love,
From these dark, dismal climes away, to cloudless scenes above;
From Sodom's ashen apples, unto fruit of endless joy,
To pleasures that will never fade, to sweets that will not cloy ;
To holy, heavenly scenes that fill the heart with happiness,
Thou drawest us, O Saviour, who around Thy footstool press.

Thou drawest us, O Saviour, by Thy word of love and peace,
That sweetly tells of joy sublime that death will but increase ;
Thou drawest us by sorrow's might, in lowliness of heart,
To cling unto Thy precious love, and choose that better part ;
Thou drawest us most sweetly by the still small voice of love,
To plume our earth-tied wings and soar on to Thy home above.

Thou drawest us, O Saviour, when the aching heart within
Broods sadly o'er its deepened stains of agony and sin ;
Thou drawest us when those we love depart, or change, or die :
No coldness gathers in Thy heart, or dims Thy loving eye.
Thou drawest us when hopes are crushed, and gloomy clouds arise ;
Thou drawest us to fix our hearts beyond the azure skies.

Thou drawest us, dear Saviour! O, 'tis sweet to come to Thee,
The ever-flowing Fount of Love, the changeless and the free,
To rest our weary, aching hearts upon Thy pitying breast,
And in the everlasting arms from every grief to rest!
Draw us still closer, Holy Friend, until, life's warfare past,
We bring our ransomed spirits at Thy sacred feet to cast.

The Fear-storm.

HAST ever *seen* the fear-storm? How around the gloomy heaven
It flings a pall of blackness from which all joy is driven;
How wrathfully it gathers, in its wild, destroying power,
O'er shrinking heads that bend where'er its clouds of terror lower!
How fails the strongest, bravest heart before the hopeless night!
How longs the trembling spirit for a glimmering ray of light!

Hast ever *heard* the fear-storm? O, how deep its thunders are,
As through the future's cavern it comes rolling from afar!
How does it shake the earth beneath the traveller's faltering feet,
And bring its wild, terrific sounds above his head to meet!
How beat the din and discord on his heated, weary brain!
How longs he for a mightier power to bring sweet peace again!

Hast ever *felt* the fear-storm? Did it ever beat on thee,
And crush the bounding spirit's joy, and bend the feeble knee?
And has it wrapped thee all around with its relentless band,
And chilled the life-blood at thy heart and paralysed thy hand?
And hast thou longed, and, longing, hast thou turned aside to pray,
That some bright Sun would rise and chase the fear-storm from thy
    way?

Ay, thou hast known the storm of fear—perchance the sickening dread
Is on thy restless spirit now.   O ! whither hast thou fled ?
There *is* a Rock of safety, and there *is* a Sun of light ;
There is a Voice almighty that can turn to day thy night.
O, while the fear-storm rageth, to that Saviour-friend draw nigh,
And rest beneath His perfect peace, until it passeth by.

The Dying Christian.

FADING are earth's pleasant things,
With its fair imaginings ;
Those best loved have passed away
Into bright, unfading day ;
And I yearn for deeper love :
Jesus, welcome me above.

Pleasures seem but trifles now ;
Holy hands have soothed my brow ;
Forms of light are floating near ;
Heavenly sounds my spirit cheer :
Dear Redeemer, be Thou nigh,
And I will not fear to die.

Ah! this change is surely death—
Fainter, shorter grows my breath ;
Shadows steal across my sight ;
Darkness deepens—give me light !
Saviour, Thou hast died before ;
Aid me till this strife is o'er.

See, my strength begins to fail :
I have entered death's dark vale ;
Rough and cold is Jordan's wave ;
Strong the arm that now can save.
Yet I calmly trust in Thee—
Highest, Holiest, be with me.

Yonder is my shining home ;
Angels beckon me to come.
Ah ! there are no shadows now,
Glory shines around my brow !
Friends on earth, farewell, farewell !
Christ is here, and all is well.

Sunshine after Rain.

THANK God for the blessed sunshine
  That cometh after rain ;
For the golden sheen is on the lea,
  And the skies are bright again.

The merry birds are singing ;
  And flowers of brilliant hue
Look up, as 'twere in thankfulness,
  To the heaven's radiant blue.

Thank God for the blessed sunshine !
  Hark ! hark to the shout and song
That are sweetly swelling upward
  As the white corn waves along.

For we look on the smiling harvest,
    On the plenty everywhere;
And the hymn of praise is rising
    Through the soft and perfumed air.

Thank God for the blessed sunshine!
    Far better than our fears
Is the kindly hand that feeds us,
    And stays the springing tears.

And the fruits of earth so precious
    Shall be gathered in again;
For our God will keep His promise
    Of the sunshine after rain.

"My Soul Thirsteth for Thee."

Psalm lxiii. 1.

Above the desert, parched and dry,
    The cloud hangs heavily;
My spirit for the Fount of Life
    Cries in its agony:
Amid the dearth, and woe, and grief,
    My God, I thirst for Thee!

The streams that glide so pleasantly,
    Beside some pilgrim feet,
Flow not beside my scorching way,
    Nor make my journey sweet:
My spirit is athirst for *Thee*,
    In whom all pleasures meet.

The gay and happy cannot halt
　Upon their gladsome way,
To throw across my cheerless night
　The sunshine of their day;
But Thou, O God, Thou lovest well
　With suffering ones to stay.

Thou heal'st the spirit's agony,
　Thou soothest the distressed;
And Thou wilt draw the weary to
　Repose upon Thy breast:
They cannot be alone or sad
　Whom Thy great love hath blest.

I thirst for Thee, my God!　O, pour
　Into my empty heart
Thy mighty, satisfying love,
　To stay its yearning smart;
"I shall be *satisfied* when I
　Am with Thee where Thou art."

Autumnal Scenes.

SOFTLY upon the sodden ground the faded leaflets lay,
And softly through a cottage home, warmed by affection's ray,
Arose the vesper song of praise from voices sweet and low,
A humble, heartfelt incense to the God who loved them so.
For summer wanderings were o'er, and absent ones had come
To kneel around that gladsome hearth, to dwell in love at home;
And hearts and eyes were uttering, as rose the evening rhyme:
" Bless God for sparing us to see this welcome autumn-time!"

There walked, with silent step, a youth beneath the branches bare,
Whose spirit listened for a voice that floated in the air :
The stars seemed holy to him then, for every step he trod
Bore written characters of truth fresh from the pen of God ;
And deeply through his kindling soul arose the vow to heaven—
" Lord, I will give myself to Thee, who all to me hast given ;
Grant that my life, like this blest hour, may with Thy love be bought,
And I will bless Thee evermore for this autumnal thought."

Upon the well-trod pavement fell the first white flakes of snow ;
A mother called her little ones, and spoke in accents low
Of hungry, houseless children, whose young hearts were aching yet
With many a long-felt sorrow that they never could forget.
She told them how the Saviour loves to see the cheerful gift,
And smiles upon the hands that strive from grief's dark depths to lift :
And forth, with kinder, warmer hearts, the children passed away,
To practise the sweet lesson they had learnt that autumn day.

Long months upon a bed of pain a fragile girl had lain,
And patiently had borne her meed of weariness and pain ;
But when the flowerets faded, and her spirit weaker grew,
The angels from the better land around her bedside drew.
Light, such as earth could never yield, shone on her heart and brow ;
Darkness will never come again ; she is with Jesus now.
All tedious, but for His deep love, would seem the summer hours,
But autumn brought her perfect peace—she faded with the flowers !

We see not yet what autumn scenes are looming o'er our way :
We know not how to us will pass this season of decay !
The autumn winds may seem for us all mournfully to sigh,
And ere the year has passed away we or our friends may die.
No matter—love is infinite ; and we may safely hide
In those kind arms of mercy where no danger can betide ;
For then, if life be long or short, the autumn hours will bring
A deeper joy than ever comes amid the flowers of spring.

Lord and Saviour, hear us!

When the choral song is pealing,
When the gathered crowd is kneeling,
And the blended prayer is stealing,
Lord and Saviour, hear us!

That our hearts to Thee uplifted,
May of every sin be sifted,
And our spirits heavenward drifted,
Lord and Saviour, hear us

When in secret sadness pining,
At Thy sacred feet reclining,
Panting for Thy love's bright shining,
Lord and Saviour, hear us!

For a spirit meek and lowly,
Loving right and goodness solely,
Like Thyself, Thou high and holy,
Lord and Saviour, hear us'

When life's duties are before us,
And the world's strong din is o'er us,
Deadening the heavenly chorus,
Lord and Saviour, hear us!

For Thy smile above us gleaming,
And a life for ever beaming
Piety, not merely *seeming*,
Lord and Saviour, hear us !

When the few last hours are flying,
And the fragile frame is dying,
Hear the spirit's feeble crying—
    Lord and Saviour, hear us!

For a life that is not fleeting
in the land of holy meeting,
Thee and all our dear ones greeting,
    Lord and Saviour, hear us!

The Father's Blessing.

"Bless me, even me also, O my Father."—Gen. xxvii. 39.

My Father! many, many prayers
    My heart has breathed to Thee;
But this, when other words were weak,
    Has sought Thee constantly;
Whate'er thou shalt deny, O give
    Thy blessing unto me.

I ask Thee not that fame or power
    May make me high or great:
Or e'en that other joys than these
    Around my path may wait;
Or any earthly sphere or boon,
    My spirit may elate.

No! Father, no! I turn from all,
    And only ask Thee now
That Thy rich blessing ever be
    Around me as I bow,
Thy precious peace within my heart,
    Thy light upon my brow.

M

Seal me as Thine, and own me, Lord,
  Wherever I may go;
Let all who know and love me here
  More of my Father know;
And grant that nought but love from mine
  To other hearts may flow.

Make me a blessing. Thou canst light
  The eye with heavenly fire;
And Thou this lisping tongue of mine
  With life-words canst inspire.
O, bless my mission everywhere;
  Grant me my heart's desire!

O, that some spirit to Thy love
  May through my prayers awake—
Some drooping sufferer cheerfully
  The sacred pathway take.
Make me a blessing, God of love!
  Bless me, for Jesus' sake.

———

Guide me, my Father.

GUIDE me, my Father! Thickly falls the night
  Around my head!
My heart is weary for the blessed light;
  The path I tread
May be the dark, drear vista of the tomb,
For it is hidden in the gathering gloom.

Guide me, my Father! Other arms are weak
  To lean upon!
The strong and mighty Comforter I seek;
  All else is gone!

O, for the everlasting arms to be
In my deep weakness closely wrapped round me!

Guide me, my Father! Aching heart and head
    Yearn for Thy breast—
Throb for the kindly hand, which erst has led,
    To give me rest:
And o'er my boding, trembling spirit fling
The holy shade of Thy protecting wing.

Guide me, my Father, or my feet will stray
    From Thee, my God—
Will, faltering, leave the strait and thorn-strewed way
    Which Jesus trod;
I would be with Him where the holy meet;
O, Friend Omnipotent, guide Thou my feet!

Guide me, my Father! Take my outstretched hand
    And lead me on,
Until the mists and pitfalls of this land
    Are ever gone;
Until my spirit is at rest with Thee,
From these dark griefs and dangers ever free.

Sin and Grace.

"Where sin abounded, grace did much more abound."—Rom. v. 20.

WHAT has sin done? Ask the battle-slain,
Or the burning lava on Sodom's plain;
List to the shriek of the widowed heart;
See the eye of the martyr start.
It has rolled o'er the streets in a mighty flood,
And deluged proud cities with noble blood.

What has sin done ?   Hear the stifled moan
Of the wretched outcast, sad and lone ;
See the darkened stain on the youthful brow,
Not bright, and fair, and cloudless now :
See the vice and squalor in wretched homes,
And the breaking hearts beneath lofty domes.

But *grace* is given.   What has *it* done ?
It has cheered the lone, forsaken one ;
It has raised the fallen to life and light ;
It has made the darkened pathway bright :
'Tis peopling heaven with the saved and free,
And scattering joy from sea to sea.

Thanks unto God for His precious gift,
Thanks unto Jesus, who thus doth lift
Our sin-stained earth from its depth of woe,
Who healeth the breaches of sin below ;
Where sin hath abounded may grace abound—
May sin-stained souls at the Cross be found !

Our Heavenly Home.

There are partings here, and the bright eyes dim,
As we sing in sadness our farewell hymn ;
But courage ! our Father's house is fair,
And hearts are not wrung by partings *there*.

There is sickness here, and the throbbing head
Tosses in pain on the sleepless bed ;
Look upward ! our Father's house is near,
And sickness may never venture *there*.

There is labour here, and the weary one
Sighs that the toil is not yet done ;
But a voice from home fills the balmy air—
The weary ones all are resting *there.*

Our Father's house!   It will not be filled
Ere His voice of welcome our heart has thrilled.
There is room for us in that mansion fair,
Nor long will our seats be vacant there.

At home with Jesus!   O, let us press
On to that heaven of blessedness !
May all we love, when our lives are past,
Meet in our Father's house at last!

The Christian's Present Rest.

"We which have believed do enter into rest."—Heb. iv. 3.

How rage the storms of life around our dwelling!
    How noisily the tempest cometh on!
How mournfully the wind its sighs is swelling!
    Can there be rest until these storms are gone?

How rapidly life's labours cluster round us!
    How the frame bends beneath its weight of toil!
How has the weariness of working bound us !
    Can there be rest upon this curse-marked soil?

Yes, even now and here is sometimes given
    A glimpse, a taste of that eternal rest
Which is awaiting us at home in heaven—
    Which we shall take on the Belovèd's breast!

Not the full sweetness of that blest reposing,
  But a faint earnest of what is to be,
That floats above us when the day is closing,
  And leaves the spirit from its sorrow free.

It is the soul unto its life-source breathing—
  It is the Saviour's holy word of peace :
'Tis when His light the aching brow is wreathing,
  Earth's gloomy weariness and sorrow cease.

O, precious, precious rest ! And if its sweetness
  Is to the weary one so precious here,
What will it be, when, robed in heavenly meetness,
  By the still waters we in heaven appear !

"He satisfieth the longing soul."

Psalm cvii. 9.

THE spirit's wailing
Reaches God's throne ; and, there prevailing,
  He sends it from the sunny skies
  The heavenly bread that satisfies ;
And the free soul, in its deep, bounding gladness,
  Forgets its sadness.

All-wise and tender
That heart of love ! He best can render
  The bread, the wine the *heart* doth crave ;
  And He the heated brow can lave
In the clear streams of His love's wasteless fountain
  From Calvary's mountain.

O, the wild thirsting!
Oft the sad heart amid its bursting
Has gone to Him in all its care,
And breathed the low, sweet breath of prayer;
And the bright blessings from the Father thronging
Have stilled the longing.

Thus, 'mid our weakness,
Father, we come to Thee in meekness;
Our empty hearts before Thee lie;
O, satisfy us, or we die;
Throw round us bonds of love no change can sever—
Be with us ever!

The Dying.

THE dying are around us everywhere!
No form so beautiful, but in the heart
That yet so fondly clings to all things fair,
There is a whisper, " Soon I must depart."
And every spot the willing feet have pressed
Is not our fatherland—is not our rest.

Bright eyes that beam upon us soon will close,
And quenched for ever be the merry breath;
The graceful limbs will lie in deep repose,
The voice of music will be hushed in death;
Silent and cold the heart—all sufferings o'er—
The blue-veined temples throb with pain no more:

O! when that marble form before us lies,
If memory of our own unkindness tells—
If dark and sad remembrances arise,
If recollection the deep sorrow swells—

How gladly would we all our treasures give
For time to cry in agony, " *Forgive !* "

If we have planted thorns within that breast,
  If bitter words were spoken in that ear,
If scorn or carelessness disturbed the rest,
  If deeds of ours have forced the burning tear,
If we have filled that heart with keen distress—
God pity us in our deep wretchedness!

If we regarded not that pleading eye,
  Nor spoke the low, sweet, healing word of love,
Nor sought in tenderness to stay the sigh,
  Nor bade the drooping spirit soar above;
If we withheld the meed of love's relief,
'Twill be the worst to bear of all our grief.

The dying are around us everywhere;
  O, to remember it each day we live,
To act, and speak, and look with kindly care,
  The ready sympathy and aid to give,
To check the careless tone and hasty breath—
So have no vain regrettings after death!

Abiding under the shadow of the Almighty.

Psalm xci. 1.

UNDER the shadow when noon-tide is shining;
Under the shadow when day is declining;
Under the shadow when sorrow is pressing;
Under the shadow when laden with blessing;

Under the shadow when loneliness saddens ;
Under the shadow when company gladdens ;
Under the shadow when joy has departed ;
Under the shadow when blithe and light-hearted ;

Under the shadow when sickness has bound us ;
Under the shadow when health is around us ;
Under the shadow if smiling or sighing ;
Under the shadow if living or dying ;

Under Thy shadow, O bountiful Father !
Under Thy shadow Thy weary ones gather ;
Under Thy shadow harm comes to us never ;
Under Thy shadow may we be for ever !

None but Jesus.

NONE but Jesus ! Every light
Fades before the gloom of night,
But this one bright star alone,
Guiding ever to the throne !
Other joys, and loves, and friends
Change before the life-tide ends ;
But the Saviour cannot die :
None but Christ can satisfy.

None but Jesus 'mid the rush
Of the world's wide whirl and crush :
He alone can still the heart
When the throbs of anguish start ;
He alone can stay the fear
When the trial hovereth near ;
He alone can succour give :
None but Jesus while we live !

None but Jesus can supply
Grace to live and grace to die ;
None but He prepare for heaven ;
He alone life's crown has given.
When the waves of conscience roll
O'er the startled, guilty soul, ˙
Only Jesus' precious blood
Can obtain us peace with God.

None but Jesus when the breath
Stops before the hand of death ;
Through the darkness dense and deep,
O, may Jesus near us keep !
None but Jesus in the land
Where the white-robed ransomed stand :
May our place with them be given,
None but Christ to praise in heaven !

Spring-time.

BEAUTIFUL Spring-time ! We hail thee now
With the chaplet of flowers upon thy brow,
With thy carpet of velvet so rich and fair,
With the floating clouds and the balmy air,
With the joyous warbling of each gay bird,
And the budding tree-tops by zephyrs stirred.

Beautiful Spring-time ! Thou seem'st to fling
Gladness and health upon everything,
Yet with the sighs of thy gentle breast
A lesson full solemn thou whisperest—
That even the light of thy sunniest day
Silently, silently fadeth away.

Beautiful Spring-time! If we might be
Joyous, and useful, and pure as thee,
We should not shrink from the fading time,
Sure of a home in a fadeless clime.
God of the seasons! O, safely bring
Our hearts to the land where 'tis always spring.

Pray for thy Loved Ones.

PRAY in the morning, when first thy thought
Turns to them with affection fraught;
In the midst of thy duties throughout the day,
When all thou canst do is to think and pray;
In the soft, sweet hour when the shadows fall,
And the twilight deepens, then pray for all.

Pray when the glance of the beaming eye
Tells its sweet language so lovingly,
When the flood of affection shall o'er thee sweep,
And thy feelings for words grow far too deep,
Breathe the emotion in fervent prayer,
And a purer bliss shall enfold thee there.

Pray for thy loved ones when far apart
From the kind, warm hand, the gentle heart;
Think of that One who is ever near;
And ask that ye each may to Him be dear;
And thy spirit-yearnings for human love
Will be more than stayed by that Friend above.

Yes, pray—for the friendships and loves of earth
Are but fragile flowers of exotic birth;

It needs that a stronger than mortal hand
Guide and protect in the wintry land;
Pray that God's blessing may still be given—
Pray that ye meet and love on in h

The Love of Jesus.

"Having loved his own which were in the world, he loved them
unto the end."—John xiii. 1.

O, LOVE of Jesus; measureless and deep,
  How far it is beyond our highest thought!
Tender and pitiful whene'er we weep,
  And ever with sweet consolation fraught.
O, heart of Jesus! what can equal Thee,
With perfect love, unchanging, boundless, free?

Ah! *Thou hast loved Thine own!* For Thou hast been
  Along the path we wearily now tread,
And Thou hast "borne our sorrows," and hast seen
  The spirit's anguish and the faint heart's dread;
And from our souls there cannot come a groan
Which finds no echo, Jesus, in Thine own!

And though Thou dost not take us to Thy home,
  Far from the world's wild wickedness and woe,
Yet that Thou seest us every day we roam,
  And lov'st us, is enough for us to know;
For Thou who changest not wilt be our Friend,
Guiding and loving till our journey's end.

Only a Step.

ONLY a step to take;
Lead me for Jesus' sake.
  Guide of my life!
Onward I still must go
Through this dark vale below,
  Clouded with strife.

Only a step I see
What is awaiting mo
  On through the way.
Dense is the atmosphere,
Danger perchance is near,
  Still as I stray.

Only a step, and then
How shall I cross the fen
  Through the dark night?
Only a step, but God
All through the way I trod
  Gave me His light.

Only a step; and He
Ever is leading me;
  Therefore I sing.
On His kind arm I'll lean.
Through every future scene,
  Close to Him cling.

Only a step may be
Left of the path for me
  Where I may roam;
Soon will the morning break—
Only a step to take
  On to my home.

"There shall be no flight there."

Rev. xxii. 5.

No night in heaven! *There* the sun's declining
　Will not disperse the happy company;
The hands and hearts that have been intertwining
　Are severed not in that society:
No passing hours sound there the parting knell;
Lips blanch not there while faltering farewell.

No night of darkness! *There* will be no groping
　With sickening spirit o'er the uncertain way;
No heart grow weary with its vain, vain hoping
　That day will break and shadows flee away;
No moan of anguish for delaying light
In that sweet resting-place where all is bright.

No night of terror! *There* no tempest-flashes
　Burst in their fury o'er a trembling world:
No earthquake's might, no awful thunder's crashes,
　No weeping o'er fair things to ruin hurled;
No scenes to rend the heart with wild despair!
No pestilence to walk in darkness there.

No night of dying! *There* they grow not weary
　Of tedious hours of sickness and of pain;
No steps to take along the "valley" dreary:
　Those dark, dark times will not return again.
The eyes will never more grow weak and dim
That God has once unclosed to look on Him.

No night in heaven! There, in lovingkind.ness,
  God smiles, and that is all the light they need:
O that it shone upon our painful blindness!
  O that that glory were for us indeed!
Dear Saviour, guide us by Thy shining light
Till *we* are safe where there is no more night!

Rain at Eventide.

How gently falls the rain! How softly sink
Into the thirsty earth these heaven-sent draughts!
How will the pencilled flowers spring up anew
And laugh in their bright beauty! There will come
Fragrance and health for every drop. How fresh
The green young leaves will be for giving it
A momentary resting-place! And birds
Will sing more sweetly for the grateful shower.
We can but think of that unwearied hand
That "watereth the earth" in its deep need,
"Making it soft with showers." And in our hearts
Rise loving, thankful thoughts of Him who gives
Water, and sun, and *love* to fructify
This God-blessed world of ours.

                  But ah! the rain
May fall upon some roofs 'neath which are hearts
Aching and sorrowful! We thank thee, Lord,
For the up-springing fount of joy and love
Within our spirits. Give to those who thirst
Draughts from the same deep well; and cheer the soul
As Thou hast blessed the sod—with drops of love
From Thy large heart of tenderness. May those
Who weep o'er blighted hopes and faded loves

See that their tear-drops watered heavenly flowers
To beautify their paths!

And if to-night,
Homeless and friendless, in the chilly street
There wander shrinking sufferers, Saviour, speak,
And to the shelter of Thy bosom draw
The wretched, lonely ones.

That blessed wing!
That secret place of the Most High! O, take
Beneath its sacred shadow us and those
Dearer than life and love! Father of all,
This night, and ever, hide us from the storm,
Till we are safely housed, far, far beyond
The rain-cloud and the darkness—*safe with Thee!*

Love-Drawings.

"With lovingkindness have I drawn thee."—Jer. xxxi. 3.

YES! it is even so! O, loving Friend,
  I, weary, wandered far away from Thee,
Almost contented my whole life to spend
  'Mid fading joys that lead to misery;
Thy hand spread blessings for my daily lot,
And yet, amid them all, I loved Thee not!

My weak, vain heart could feast on meaner charms—
  Could drink the world's poor "broken cisterns" dry.
I flew for rest and peace to other arms,
  Nor stayed to wonder who was standing nigh,
Until in mercy, measureless and free,
Thy lovingkindness drew me unto Thee!

There was no earthquake's might, no thunder's roar,
  No stern command to strike with terror's power;
No flashing, fiery sword was hanging o'er,
  No fierce avengers thronged around that hour;
No dreadful terrors sent my soul to meet,
And drag me trembling, cowering, to Thy feet.

A smiling eye looked tenderly on me,
  A still small voice came sweetly o'er my soul;
That look, that voice, I knew they were from Thee,
  And to Thine open arms I gently stole;
O Father, Friend, I bless Thee for that hour:
Thy lovingkindness was resistless power!

And now I ask Thee, if my changing heart
  Should wander from Thy resting-place again,
O, draw me back to that far better part—
  Thy lovingkindness cannot speak in vain.
Thine, only Thine, for ever I would be;
O! " draw me, and I will run after Thee."

Pray when the Daylight Fadeth.

Pray when the daylight fadeth, for perchance on silent wings
The angels float about thee then and breathe of holy things;
The calm upon thy spirit, that with twilight's hour is given,
O, has it not a mission from the brighter scenes in heaven?

Pray when the daylight fadeth, that the freshly-gathered sin
Be wiped by Jesus' hands away ere darker hours begin;
That He in tenderness may cleanse the earth-stain from thy brow,
And wrap the mantle of His love closely around thee now.

N

Pray when the daylight fadeth : after all its restless care
'Tis well to calm the trembling soul with soothing words of prayer ;
To stay the spirit's yearnings with the Saviour's deathless love,
And 'mid the shadows catch a glimpse of a better world above.

Pray when the daylight fadeth, that the sombre hours of night
May bring a deeper peace to thee than e'en the gladsome light.
Pray that, when life's last eventide shall fall upon thy way,
A radiant messenger may lead thee forth to endless day.

A Happy New Year.

I WISH you, dear reader, a happy new year,
Amid all that is hopeful, and bright, and dear;
'Mid scenes about which thy spirit dreams,
Where the star of affection brightly beams ;
And numberless blessings be richly given
By the bountiful hand of the God of Heaven.

It may be, dear reader, that thou art one
Toiling from morn till the setting sun,
Or one of the noble of our land,
Holding the paper with jewelled hand;
But the rich and the poor need happiness,
And I pray that our Father alike may bless.

If thou art young, may the coming year
Be made more bright for thy sojourn here ;
May loftier aims, and a holier strife,
Dignify ever thy buoyant life,
And place thee, whatever may be thy birth,
With the really good and great of earth.

Or, if thou art now in thy manhood's prime,
May a purer glory illume thy time;
And thy fearless heart, and thy lofty brow,
Learn at the feet of thy God to bow;
And long ere the flashing eye grow dim,
May all that thou art be alone for Him.

Or, if thou art aged and weak become,
God guide thee gently towards thy home,
Gather thee tenderly to His breast,
In the home where the weary ones may rest,
Where the bloom of youth is renewed again,
And the air ne'er echoes with sounds of pain.

God bless you all with a title clear
To the land where 'tis *ever* a happy year;
And then, should this, with its joy and mirth,
Be the last we are spared to spend on earth,
We'll joyfully welcome the summons given
To meet dear friends in our home—in heaven!

Christians of all Sects, Unite!

CHRISTIANS! listen to the voices
    Echoing on either hand;
Look around you—clouds are breaking—
    Light is spreading o'er the land.
Happier, holier days are coming,
    They will sweetly dawn at length;
Christians! only be united—
    Union ever will be strength.
Speed the day of Gospel light—
Christians of all sects, unite!

Lay aside all party feeling,
Hating only what is wrong;
Aim to elevate the masses
Who in darkness suffered long;
Urge them in your love and kindness
To embrace the brotherhood:
Help, and hinder not each other,
Never check the cause of good;
Know ye not that right is might?
In love's enterprise unite!

Christians! ever work together
In the Gospel harvest-field,
Fighting only against evil,
With a power that will not yield.
Following one glorious Leader,
Striving for one victory,
Surely ye should love each other—
Surely ye should brethren be.
O! it were a glorious sight
If ye would but all unite!

Yonder, looming in the distance,
Is your one oft-longed-for home;
And the universal Father
Ever onward bids you come.
Why not now commence the greeting?
Why not let the Gospel flame
Burn intensely, thus consuming
All dislike and party name?
Welcome on th' approaching light—
Christians of all sects, unite!

The Day's Rejoicing.

"Thou makest the outgoings of the morning and evening to
rejoice."—Psalm lxv. 8.

" THOU makest the *morning* rejoice." In its gladness
It pours its bright beams o'er the beautiful earth,
That shakes off its shadows of slumber and sadness,
And wakes with its thrill of wild pleasure and mirth.

" Thou makest the morning rejoice," and up-springing
From strength-giving sleep do Thy children arise;
Glad hearts beating time to the songs they are singing—
The matins of love soaring up to the skies.

"Thou makest the *evening* rejoice," for Thou spreadest
The curtain of darkness o'er tree-top and flower.
Thou visitest earth, and wherever Thou treadest,
Thy works bless Thee still for the soft, peaceful hour.

" Thou makest the evening rejoice;" for, O Father,
How sweet to the weary the season of rest!
How welcome the stillness with which Thou dost gather
To sleep and refreshment the sad and oppressed!

We thank Thee, O God, for the joy Thou art giving,
At morn and at eventide blessing us still;
May we, who rejoice in it, ever be living
To love Thee and serve Thee, performing Thy will.

Need.

"Your Father knoweth that ye have need of these things."—
Luke xii. 30.

NEED of the water and the daily bread
    That fresh with morning and with evening fall.
Our Father knoweth that we must be fed,
    And gives ere lisping lips for blessing call.

Need of the daily discipline of life—
    The trial sharp ; the difficulty deep ;
The rough encounter in the deadly strife ;
    The constant weariness to sweeten sleep.

Need of the sun athwart the sky to shine ;
    Need of the flowers to blossom by the way ;
Need of the love around our hearts to twine ;
    Need of the joy t' irradiate the day.

And with no grudging heart, no meagre hand,
    Our Father giveth us the good we need ;
His gifts fall broadcast o'er the hungry land :
    Praise unto God, for His is love indeed.

Guidance.

" Thou shalt guide me with thy counsel, and afterward receive me
to glory."—Psalm lxxiii. 24.

DIM the path of life appears,
Shaded oft by grief and fears ;
And around my trembling feet
Many difficulties meet :
All uncertain is my way,
Father, guide me, lest I stray.

Thine the counsel that I seek,
To uphold and cheer the weak ;
Other wisdom cannot be
Equal to directing me ;
Father, guide me where to go,
Lead in paths I do not know.

Only let my footsteps tend
Where all griefs and transport end ;
To Thy glory, O receive,
Never more my God to leave :
Kindly, softly, guide me home,
Where my feet can never roam.

The Fountain of Life.

"Whosoever will, let him take the water of life freely."—Rev. xxii. 17.

LIFE in the desert, a thirsty land,
Longings and yearnings on every hand!
Praise for the Fountain that ever springs,
Showering its drops o'er earth's drooping things.
Bringing fresh hopes to the fainting soul,
Making the weary and wounded whole.

Traveller, toiling up life's steep hill,
Linger not long in the shallow rill ;
Haste to the Fountain ! it gushes high
With the waters of immortality ;
Traveller, thirst by the way no more,
Drink at the streams that are running o'er.

Thou who comest with youthful mien,
Bright is thy future, thy path serene ;
Yet are there times when thou thirstest still,
When the broken cisterns all fail to fill,
When thy spirit yearns for a purer joy,
Which grows not dim and will never cloy.

Thou who hast drunk at each other stream,
Gliding along with its sunny gleam,
Turning from each one dissatisfied,
Mourning to find them so often dried,
Thine are the cravings too deep for earth,
And the aspirings of loftier birth.

Freely the Fountain is flowing on ;
Traveller, come ere thy life be gone.
Here are the waters that never dry,
Here is the good that will satisfy ;
Come, ere the day and its heat are o'er ;
Drink of the Fountain, and thirst no more.

Immortality.

" Whosoever liveth and believeth in me shall never die."—John xi. 26.

" SHALL never die ! "   Across the tearless eye
    Shall come no shadow of disease or pain ;
The limbs in helplessness no more shall lie,
    Nor pulses throb in agony again ;
The spirit ne'er grow weary in its flight,
Once living in that land of deathless light.

O ! sometimes through these scenes of mournful shade,
  The cypresses of this dark wilderness,
There come faint streaks of that unwaning sun,
  The pilgrim's dark and dangerous way to bless,
The heart's impatience to rebuke and quell,
By thoughts of heaven, where peace and pleasure dwell.

"Shall never die !"   Live through eternity,
  Amid unchanging scenes, and loves, and friends,
Singing sweet angel-songs that never tire,
  Where the day's pleasure neither cloys nor ends.
To be immortal, O my spirit, rise !
Thy native country is beyond the skies.

The Neglected Friend.

"But thou hast not called upon me, O Jacob; but thou hast been weary of me,
O Israel."—Isaiah xliii. 22.

THERE is an eye that o'er thy path has bent its loving gaze ;
A hand whose power has guided thee through all its rugged ways ;
Kind arms that have enfolded thee when storms have beaten wild ;
A heart that loves more tenderly than mother does her child.
But all the untold depths of love that in *thy* spirit dwell
Have not been poured before His feet who loveth thee so well !

Fragile and weak, thy steps have paced, with hesitating feet,
The path where many dangers throng and thorns and briars meet.
He planted flowers all fresh and fair at every step to spring,
And made the way so pleasant that thou couldst but stay and sing ;
His tokens of affection thou didst gladly stoop to cull,
All careless of the loving hand that made them beautiful.

The deep, deep heart He gave thee yearned for friendship's precious
    meed,
He sent thee fond and faithful friends to meet thy spirit's need;
With passionate devotion thou didst learn to them to cling,
The clasping tendrils of thy heart round human props to fling;
But to that One Almighty Friend whose love no change could dim,
Ah, thou hast grown indifferent, and cold, and tired of Him.

There was deep terror all around—the noisome pestilence
Breathed out its subtile, poisoned breath, while crowds were hurried
    hence;
It came not nigh His cherished one, for o'er thy guarded head
With watchful love and tenderness His shielding wing was spread.
A passing thought thou gavest Him, then careless turned away,
And when the danger fled forgot who thus had been thy stay.

And yet He is unchanging still! O, by His mighty love,
Forget not Him who claims thy heart all other friends above.
Go to Him in thy weariness, He wearies not of thee;
Call on Him yet again, thou needest such a friend as He;
Wound not that tender, loving heart—then, when all ties are riven,
Life, joy, security, and peace shall with that Friend be given.

Flowers.

FLOWERS, bright flowers! They are everywhere
Filling with fragrance the laden air,
Smiling in hedgerow and garden bower,
Wooing the sunbeam and gentle shower,
Painting the earth in a thousand dyes,
Pointing for aye to the azure skies.

Flowers, bright flowers! How we love them all,
For the joyous thought which their names recall!
How oft does the gift of a flow'ret tell
Tales which the lips could not breathe so well,
Tales of friendship and human love,
Tales of a holier Friend above!

Flowers, bright flowers! O, this world of ours
Is passing rich with its wealth of flowers!
And 'tis sweet to think, if a Father's care
Makes our place of sojourn here so fair,
What beauty must rest on everything
In our lasting home of eternal spring!

" Pray without Ceasing."

1 Thess. v. 17.

When the sun of prosperity shines on thy path,
    And illumines the flower-clad way,
Or sorrow has clouded the prospect of joy—
    O! stop in thy journey and pray.

When friends are around thee, with kindness and smiles,
    Thy heart with new pleasure to thrill,
Or when they have left thee bereaved and alone—
    O! worship the Mightiest still.

Whene'er thou art entering an untrodden way,
    O! linger awhile on the sod;
Look upward for guidance and strength in thy need;
    In all things acknowledge thy God.

And still, for the duties that cluster around
  Each hour as it passes away,
There is need in the trifling events of our lives
  To remember our Father and pray.

For gladness is deepened to exquisite joy,
  And lighter grow sorrow and care,
If our spirits ascend to their Maker and God
  In the hallowed engagement of prayer!

"O Lord, revive thy Work.

Hab. iii. 2.

FATHER, from Thy throne in heaven
  Hear the prayer our spirits frame;
O, revive Thy work amongst us,
  Spread the knowledge of Thy name.
Vain is every human effort,
  None can stem the tide of ill
But the hand that is Almighty:
  Bid—O! bid the waves be still.

Gather to the Gospel vineyard
  Those who ne'er have bent the knee;
Bring the strong and firm of purpose
  Earnestly to work for Thee;
Bring the young and bring the aged,
  Bring the rich and bring the poor,
Bid the healthy and afflicted
  Seek for pleasures that endure.

Cold and weak is our devotion,
  Dimly burn the altar fires,
Sinful thoughts, and words, and actions
  Clog the spirit that aspires.
All our lives are sin-encrusted,
  Guilt enshrouds this world of thine :
Holy Spirit, hear, O, hear us !
  Sun of Righteousness, O, shine !

Quicken, purify our churches,
  Make Thy children love Thee more,
Let the thoughtless congregation
  Know Thee, serve Thee, and adore.
Let our homes be sweetly lighted
  With the sunshine of Thy love ;
Let our hearts, with every feeling,
  Ever turn to Thee above.

Gloriously Thy truth is spreading,
  Wide and far in other lands ;
Surely Thou wilt bless *our* nation,
  And increase its Christian bands.
Hear, O, hear us, heavenly Father !
  Make us earnest when we pray ;
O, revive Thy work among us ;
  Hasten on the Gospel day.

For Jesus' Sake.

FOR Jesus' sake ! At rosy morn, and in the silent night,
The band of earnest mothers press around the throne of light ;
And beg, with softly earnest lips, large blessings from above
On the little ones their large, deep hearts have cherished with such love.

Why plead they so ? *" For Jesus' sake."* They think how once there
  pressed
Children, and how He took them to His kind and sheltering breast.

" For Jesus' sake" the sorrowful in silent accents plead,
Amid the heart's intensest pain, the spirit's greatest need ;
For they know the Saviour feels for them—the " Man of Sorrows"
  knows
How best to pour the healing balm—the balsam of repose ;
And they ask, *for Jesus' sake,* to feel the deep, unshadowed peace
That soothes the storm's white-crested waves and bids its dashing
  cease.

" For Jesus' sake," the army of the King of kings, who stay
Awhile and kneel together on the rough and rugged way,
Ask for success to bless them in that all-prevailing Name
Beneath whose banner they are placed to celebrate His fame :
For He can bend the stubborn heart ; and nations, as they bow,
Pay homage to the Son of God, their Friend and Saviour now.

" For Jesus' sake !" We thank Thee, Lord, for such a mighty plea
To cast before Thy footstool, when we bring our wants to Thee ;
We thank Thee for a Friend like Him for whose dear sake we come,
And ask that, in that better home, for us there may be room.
O, let us cling to His deep love, to guide and bless us here,
And intercede for us below in yon celestial sphere.

God's Acre.

I love that ancient Saxon phrase which calls
The burial-ground God's acre.—LONGFELLOW.

YES, it is very beautiful to think
The lovely human flower, so passing dear
To our deep, yearning hearts, will only fade
To blossom with resplendent beauty in
'Th' Eternal's garden ! It is sweet to feel
That they are amaranthines, and that when
Our tearful eyes may linger not again
Upon the brow we loved too well ; nor meet
The eloquent glance which thrilled us with its love,
In love's own dialect ; nor feel the hands
That soothed and blessed us once, the Husbandman
Has only covered them that they may grow
More glorious in the everlasting spring !

God's acre. He will tend it then ! Our flowers—
Our precious flowers, and beautiful—are safe
From nipping frosts and burning, blighting winds ;
No storm can beat upon them, no hot sun
Bend their frail heads.

O, happy resting ones !
We, who are toiling here with reeking brows,
And heavy, aching hearts, oft yearn to be
Planted as ye are by the cooling wave
Of life's pure river ! When *we* wither here,
Life's scorching fever o'er, may gentle hands
Lay us beside ye in God's acre, till
He calls us forth to bloom in Paradise !

The Shelter.

"And a man shall be as an hiding-place from the wind, and a covert from the tempest; as rivers of water in a dry place, as the shadow of a great rock in a weary land."—Isaiah xxxii. 2.

When the wintry winds are blowing,
  All around is cold and drear,
Black the sky and rough the pathway,
  Nought to beautify and cheer,
Holiest, let us see Thy face,
Be our blessed hiding-place.

When the angry tempest gathers,
  When the vivid lightnings flash,
When the storm-cloud bursts above us,
  And the awful thunders crash,
Mighty God! our covert be,—
Let us hide ourselves in Thee.

When we toil o'er life's hot desert,
  Aching brow and way-worn feet,
Fainting from the thirst within us,
  Panting for the waters sweet,—
Fountain! let us drink of Thee,
Living waters rich and free.

When the hot and blistering sunshine
  Gleams upon the path we tread,
With its deep, red rays above us,
  Scorching ever heart and head,—
Rock of Ages! in Thy shade
Let Thy weary ones be laid.

Be our all while yet we linger
In this changing, shifting place;
Nearer, and yet nearer draw us,
Till we gaze upon Thy face—
Till we gain Thy blissful home,
Where the tempest cannot come.

Walking by Faith.

"By faith Abraham, when he was called to go out into a place which he should after receive for an inheritance, obeyed; and he went out, not knowing whither he went."—Heb. xi. 7.

THERE came a voice from heaven to him, that servant of the Lord,
To rise and leave his father's house and travel far abroad,—
To leave the country of his birth, the friends that loved him well,
And, in the stranger's distant land, 'mid other scenes to dwell.

With confidence unquestioning, he rose and went his way
To journey to the southern land, nor dared to disobey;
And, taking but a single step, as God directed him,
Fearless and hopefully he went along the pathway dim.

And we are following Abraham: the future's vista seems
Uncertain and mysterious as are our midnight dreams;
But still we journey on, and on, where'er our Father leads,
Through dark, intricate forest shades, or sweet and flowery meads.

He knoweth what is best for us, and so we lay our hand
In His strong grasp, and onward press toward the unseen land;
These hills and valleys in our road we've trodden not before,
But gratefully and hopefully our feet are passing o'er.

O

Sometimes the path diverges, and our weakness cannot see
How that new rugged mountain-side a better way can be;
We only know that it is right, and feel that God is there;
And trustingly go forward, for we know the end is fair!

And though the way be long, or short, we have no cause to fear
While the inheritance is sure, and our great Leader near;
We're journeying to the better land of which our God has told:
O happy day, when we at last its turrets shall behold!

"He knoweth the way that I take."

Job xxiii. 10.

THIS dark, intricate way—this strange, strange maze—
  He knoweth it, however dim it be!
His eye can penetrate the thickened haze,
  O'er trodden paths, and those awaiting me.

His presence has been with me as I trod
  O'er fens, by pitfalls, up the rough hill-side;
Wending, through dangerous paths, my way to God,
  Tended and cheered by an Omniscient Guide.

There have been poisoned arrows in the air,
  And deadly serpents waiting to destroy,
While my dim eyes saw nothing but was fair,
  And rested only on sweet things of joy.

And yet I have been safe! He knew it all,
  And hedged me in by His thick cloud of love.
How could I stumble as I walked, or fall,
  With such a power around, beneath, above?

He knoweth it! As on I journey now
  No ill can come, no blessing brightly glow,
No sunny gladness pass athwart my brow,
  But He who knows and sends it all must know.

He knoweth it! The very secret thought
  That none but He may read—the wish, the sigh,
The silent prayer with private import fraught—
  All, all are bare before that piercing eye.

Thou know'st the way I take. Then, O my God!
  Make me content the devious way to tread;
Thou who hast helped me every step I trod,
  Lead me still, Father, as Thou erst hast led.

Prepare the Living for Life.

PREPARE, O God, for life! The pulse is bounding,
  The life-blood rushes through the healthy veins,
Clear voices in Thy temple are resounding,
  And buoyant feet trip lightly o'er earth's plains.

But not for this alone Thy love is sparing;
  This is not life, as Thou wouldst have us live:
Father, prepare us to be always sharing
  The *duty* that it is Thy will to give.

For life is *labour* to the willing spirit,
  Who takes from Thee that heritage of love;
Grant that Thy living children may inherit
  The power to live as angels do above.

Prepare us, God, for life !   O, bless and strengthen
Heart, brain, and hand to labour on for Thee ;
The " silver cord of life" still kindly lengthen
Until, the "day's work done," to heaven we flee.

The Saviour's Prophecy.

" In the world ye shall have tribulation : in me ye shall have
peace."—John xvi. 33.

EACH passing day in gloomy lines is telling
How very true these words of prophecy :
However love may guard the Christian's dwelling,
Still tribulation always lurketh nigh.
The cry of sorrow may not be repressed,
Where voices whisper, This is not thy rest.

Life's characters in burning scrolls are written,
That scar the soul and purge the shrinking heart !
The weak and helpless by the scourge are smitten,
The loved and loving fall beneath the dart ;
And shrieks of anguish evermore arise,
Praying for pity from the brighter skies.

But when the Christian 'neath his load is sighing,
Soft, healing balm is scattered all around,
Voices from heaven seem to be replying,
And o'er his spirit falls a calm profound.
Rest comes to aching head, and heart, and feet,
For Jesus' peace-words are so very sweet.

"In me ye shall have peace." O, from our spirit
We breathe our prayer, dear Saviour, unto Thee
Let us this gracious legacy inherit,
    And we'll not wish from sorrow to be free.
Bid all our sinful murmurings to cease,
Help us to find in Thee this sacred peace.

"I will not leave you comfortless, I will come to you."

John xiv. 19.

THE weary, way-worn wanderer weeps upon the roughened sod,
And sometimes in his aching heart arise hard thoughts of God;
But the Saviour's promise comforts him—Ye shall not be alone,—
And his step resumes its buoyancy, his heart its lightest tone;
For the *companionship of Christ* is peace, and joy, and rest,
And a radiance from above shall gild the pathway He has pressed.

The sad and sinking sufferer, on his bed of wasting pain,
How prays he for the gladsome time when life is full again!
But O, how soft the soothing words fall on the heated head—
"I will not leave you comfortless!" And round the weary bed
Come music-strains, and cooling breeze, and life-words from above;
And the faint heart is strong again in Jesus' strength and love.

The mourning mother's wild lament—what agonizing cries
From the deep, surcharged heart ascend, and pierce the o'erhanging
    skies!
Her empty arms she upward lifts in groans of deep despair—
But Jesus hears and understands th' unspoken anguished prayer.
He does not leave her comfortless; He heals the broken heart;
He tells her they will meet again—*meet*, but shall never *part*.

"I will not leave you comfortless!"   Dear Saviour, Thou hast not;
The promise spoken long ago is not e'en now forgot;
Whatever grief befalls us, still Thou com'st to us in love;
And life, with all its din and woe, is like our home above.
O, when the load is heaviest, let us for ever flee
To the long-trusted Comforter—O! Saviour, Friend, to Thee.

Pray for the Unconverted.

PRAY for the unconverted—
  O! pass not coldly by,
Content alone to journey
  To thy home beyond the sky!
They have no hope of heaven
  To cheer their darksome night:
No angel-fingers beckon
  To the land of love and light.

Pray for them! *They* are aliens
  From the sacred commonwealth;
They share not in the blessings
  Of redemption, peace, and health;
They have no hand above them
  To remove the scalding tears;
They are not taught the music
  Of the radiant spirit-spheres.

Pray for them! They are weary;
  But they know not how to rest,
In child-like trust and safety,
  On the Redeemer's breast.

Life's tempests beat around them;
But they have not where to hide—
They have no secret dwelling
Where their spirits may abide.

Pray for the unconverted;
O! pass not coldly by,
Nor leave them in the darkness
Still, to suffer and to die!
Plead for them with thy Saviour—
He has love enough to spare;
O! lead them unto Jesus
With the holy words of prayer.

Falling Leaves.

ALL mournfully borne on the soft-sighing breeze,
The leaves of the forest are falling;
And, brought to our hearts through the desolate trees,
Deep voices are constantly calling.

Deprived of their beauty, they fall to the ground,
The wild winds their requiem sighing;
And sadly our autumn-thoughts gather around,
For we, like the leaves, are all dying.

And silently, solemnly, whisperings come—
Our summer will shortly be ended;
And we shall lie down in the damp, narrow home,
Where our feet all our life-time have tended.

But O! when we fade, may our spirits all be
To the garden of Paradise taken,
Fresh bloom and fresh fragrance and beauty to see,
When the dead from their sleep shall awaken!

The Approach to God.

"Wherewith shall I come before the Lord?"—Micah vi. 6.

Not with a heart that scarcely feels
The words that my lips repeat,
With cold, unmeaning sentences
To lay on the mercy-seat;
But a spirit low and prostrate there
Pours forth its breathings in fervent prayer.

Not with a mind that but half believes
The confessions my tongue may speak,
That scarcely allows itself to be
Wretched and vile and weak;
But a heart that feels its sinfulness,
And entreats of Thee to forgive and bless.

Not with a heart whose affection clings
To the treasures God has given,
Nor turns in its passionate fervency
And its highest hopes to heaven;
But contented to feel earth's joys grow dim,
That my God may allure me nearer Him.

Then sprinkled alone by Jesus' blood,
   And having His holiness,
I will throw me down at my Father's feet,
   And there my petitions press.
None wait in vain for His cheering voice;
He makes the desponding soul rejoice.

So whenever the path through life grows rough,
   And my spirit is faint and weak,
I will bring Him myself—just as I am,
   Sinful and vile and weak.
I know I am guilty in His sight;
But the Saviour's robe is of spotless white.

" Thou visitest the Earth."

Psalm lxv. 9.

" Thou visitest the earth." The gentle showers
   Fall softly on the dry and thirsty land;
The freshened earth is beautiful with flowers,
   And fragrant with the incense of Thy hand.
And every gem up-springing from the sod
Shows, in its pencilled tints, the love of God.

" Thou visitest the earth," and every spot,
   Wakens to boundless melody and mirth;
There is no place where Thy kind hand is not,
   And all things bless Thee on the teeming earth :
Birds, streams, and breezes warble their sweet lays
In one glad anthem to their Maker's praise.

" Thou visitest the earth," and men rejoice;
 Fountains of life at Thy glad coming spring;
The young and old arise with cheerful voice,
 Beneath the azure dome Thy love to sing,
Who makest all things beautiful and fair,
But lov'st Thy children with the fondest care.

" Thou visitest the earth." O, Father God,
 Help us, with grateful hearts, to welcome Thee;
To rev'rence each bright spot where Thou hast trod,
 And worship Thee with spirits glad and free.
O, visit us, our Father, in Thy love,
And meeten us to dwell with Thee above.

The Hushed Storm.

" Then are they glad, because they be quiet."—Psalm cvii. 30.

" HE makes the storm a calm !" The sea on which God's children sail
Is sometimes tossed in billows high before the mighty gale;
But the spirit's cry uprises to the God whose power can save,
And a wise and mighty hand is stretched to stay the stormy wave.
The tempest's rage, the billows' roar, the waters' battle cease,
And there rests upon the booming sea a solemn, silent peace.

" He makes the storm a calm !" And then the voyagers are glad
When quietness is on the sea, and heaven in sunbeams clad;
For there falls upon their spirits such a deep and tranquil love,
That e'en their dark and stormy course brings glimpses from above.
Ay, they are *glad* in joy Divine amid their quietness,
Reposing peacefully on Him whose joy it is to bless.

O, Thou who hold'st the waters in the hollow of Thy hand,
Before the tempest of Thy wrath how shall Thy children stand ?
But give us quietness and peace, and teach us how to praise
The powerful Guardian of our night, the Joy-spring of our days.
So bring us safe through wind and storm to yonder blissful place;
There clouds will never hide from us our Father's smiling face.

God's Loaf.

" Love is God's loaf, and this is that feeding for which we are taught to pray, ' Give us this day our daily bread.' "—HENRY WARD BEECHER.

" LOVE is God's loaf." The Feeder only knows
　　How very hungry is the empty heart
In which affection's nutriment ne'er flows—
　　Which bears alone its deep and anguished smart ;
And He who once the fainting thousands fed
Made for the hungry heart love's precious bread.

" Love is God's loaf." And daily there arise
　　Wailing entreaties from the burdened sod—
The universal prayer, in sobs and sighs,
　　" Give us this day our daily bread, O God'
And the All-Father listens to the cry,
And feeds His hungry children, lest they die.

" Love is God's loaf." And therefore there is given
　　Such sweet affection in this stricken earth,
Such love immortal in our home in heaven,
　　And here such fond, fond ties of home and hearth :
Love filling up the spirit's deep recess,
And twining round us but to soothe and bless.

" Love is God's loaf." *His* boundless, deathless love
Alone can satisfy the yearning heart;
Can fill with joy akin to that above,
The deep, deep spirit with its ache and smart;
Lord, evermore give us this living bread;
May we, Thy hungry ones, with love be fed!

The Wish of the Weary.

O that I had wings like a dove! for then would I fly away and be
at rest."—Psalm lv. 6.

O HAPPY dove, who its soft wing is spreading
To bear it homeward to its sheltering nest;
There's no such home for me; I must be treading
The thorny pathway where's no place of rest.

O, had I also wings, I would be flying
Swift to my own most happy home above—
Would gain that blessed rest for which I'm sighing,
Happy for ever in my Saviour's love.

As duties gather, I become more weary,
And mortal strength fails with each passing day;
Alone and weak, I climb the hill-side dreary—
O that I had but wings to fly away!

Yet stay, my spirit, cease thy sad repining:
There is a holy resting-place for thee;
There is a smile of love above thee shining,
But not to set thee from life's duties free.

No; He who knoweth best still bids me linger,
   And labour in His vineyard here below;
And I will ever watch His guiding finger,
   And where His will requireth me will go.

Let me be patient—soon my spirit's anguish
   Will find relief upon the Saviour's breast,
No more beneath life's ills to sigh and languish,
   Nor ever leave that deep and tranquil rest.

Leaning-Trusts.

Weak, fragile, ivy-like, how much we need some mighty thing
To which in all their confidence our yearning hearts may cling!
Earth gives it not; its strongest things are reeds, too well we know,
Yet round these supple things how oft our passion-grasp we throw!

Toward flattering earthly pleasures, O, how eagerly we press!
The love of human hearts, how oft 'tis all our happiness!
The praise of mortal lips, what could we dare, and do, to win!
How precious do these joys all seem! Alas! how full of sin!

'Tis very true, " He builds too low who builds below the skies;"
For when earth's fragile leaning-trusts too earnestly we prize,
While tranquilly we cling to them, and 'neath their shadow lie,
Our best-beloved, our beautiful, will droop, and fade, and die.

Yet 'tis a loving hand that casts our fairest treasures low,
And pitying eyes that watch us as our hearts despairing grow;
O Rock of Ages! teach us how afresh to Thee to cling!
O Friend above all other friends, Thy arms about us fling!

The Weary Heart.

My heart is weary of its inner life,
　　So dark, so cold, so hardened, and unclean;
So powerless for the Christian's constant strife;
　　Shrinking so cowardly from each rough scene;
So full of doubt, and dread, and murmuring;
　　So empty of the beautiful and good;
Full of complaints at every painful thing,
　　And 'mid its blessings such ingratitude.

My heart is weary of its constant sin;
　　Fresh spots accumulate each passing hour;
My spirit sickens at a glance within,
　　Where evil has such undisputed power.
Thoughts, wishes, feelings, have the same deep stain;
　　Darkly it gathers all around my life.
Sinning—repenting—sinning then again—
　　Shall I ne'er rest from all this sin and strife?

My heart is weary of its constant toil,
　　Labouring ever amid many fears,
Sowing upon a wild and fruitless soil,
　　And reaping nothing but more grief and tears;
Striving for phantoms that elude my grasp
　　Lured by the *ignis fatuus* astray;
Apples of Sodom in my tightened clasp—
　　Joys that, if bright, are brief, and fade away.

My heart is weary even of its love,
　　Pouring its deep tide forth in bitter pain;
Throwing its tendrils earthward, not above;
　　Spending its rich intensity in vain;

Leaning on frail, frail reeds, that weakly bend,
  E'en while the "Rock of Ages" is close by!
Yearning for love while the All-loving Friend
  With more than human tenderness is nigh.

My heart is weary. Jesus, Thou art rest
  To those who sigh in agony for Thee.
O, take me to Thy kind and sheltering breast,
  And calm and happy will my spirit be!
Melt, purify my hardened, sin-stained heart,
  By keeping me for ever near Thy side;
'Tis heaven to be, dear Saviour, where Thou art—
  O let the weary heart with Thee abide!

Come with us.

"We are journeying unto the place of which the Lord said, I will
  give it you; come thou with us."—Numb. x. 29.

Come, brothers, come! We're a little band,
Treading the path to our fatherland,
With hearts so glad that we march and sing,
Cheering for ever the journeying;
O! there is joy in our distant home;
Quicken your footsteps—come, brothers, come!

Come, sisters, come! There are pastures sweet,
Where the weary rest their aching feet;
Unfading flowers and a cloudless sky,
And founts of love that are never dry!
And a Father's welcome waits us there,
In our home where all is so bright and fair!

If the path be long, we've a faithful Guide
Tending us still by the rough way-side;
Up the mountain-pass—through the leafy glade—
There are clear still waters and cooling shade;
And the gentle zephyrs around us play,
As we earnestly press through the flower-clad way.

And O, what transport each spirit fills,
As we catch a glimpse of the distant hills!
Hark! there's a whisper of thrilling strains
Floating to us from the far-off plains;
Courage and joy! for we're nearing home!
Come with us, loiterers—quickly come.

A November Lay.

FAREWELL to the summer!—the bright, bright days
Have passed, with the hot sun's cloudless blaze;
Our twilight rambles through lanes are o'er,
The summer song-bird is heard no more;   ·
The wreaths of the garden fast fade away,
We love them all—but they may not stay.

Dark mists have gathered o'er mountain brows,
Cold winds are sighing through forest boughs;
Silently fall the brown leaves around,
Carpeting sadly the sodden ground;
Flowers in their beauty cheer not the sight,
And the stars shine coldly the long, long night.

Yet, welcome to winter! We hail the birth
Of the sweet, long evenings of joy and mirth;
The bright, warm hearth, with its burst of song,
And the loving ones which around it throng;
The gay, glad laugh and the smiling eye,
The thrilling look and the kind reply.

Yes, welcome to winter! May happiness
Cheer the dark days, and the fireside bless—
Joy in the dwellings where kindred meet—
No missing voices—no vacant seat—
And a hope, when these fond ties are riven,
Of a sweeter gathering at home in heaven.

Prepare the Dying for Death.

PREPARE, O God, for death those who are dying;
   Those whose life-sands have very nearly run;
Those who the last faint breath must soon be sighing,
   O'er whose dim eyes now sinks the setting sun.

Let not the mighty foe come unexpected,
   The failing pulse, the weak and fainting heart—
Let them not tremble, that they have neglected
   The preparation for the hour to part.

O, let the dying feel their sins forgiven,
   And have Thy love to light them through the flood;
So that, when these frail life-cords shall be riven,
   They may be white and fair through Jesus' blood.

P

Prepare *us*, Lord, for death, for *we* are dying;
  All suddenly Thy hand may stop our breath:
O, in that season, may we be relying
  Wholly on Thee, for Thou hast conquered death.

————

And she answered, "It is well."

YES, it is always well, O God, .
  With those who trust in Thee;
It matters not how sad or dark
  Their earthly lot may be:
For the intricate threads of life
  Are woven by Thy hand,
And every change that marks our days
  Is sent at Thy command.

'Tis well when darkness shrouds the path,
  And day's bright scenes depart;
Well, when the pang of agony
  Has riven the bleeding heart—
When to its wild, wild questionings
  There cometh no reply;
Well, when in utter helplessness
  We lay us down to die.

We know that all is well; but O!
  Amid the tempest's moan,
When fierce it rages all around,
  Let us not be alone.
Be with us, Thou, whose mighty word
  Can still the angry sea,
And, through the rough and rushing storm,
  Our " Rock " of Ages be.

For then must all be well—the fire
That comes but to refine
Will be a blessing if it make
Our souls more wholly Thine;
And when at last the feeble voice
Shall heaven's glad chorus swell,
Still then, as now, Thy children, Lord,
Will answer, " It is well."

"To be with Christ, which is far better."

Phil. i. 23.

THERE are deep and solemn warnings gathering ever round our way,
That remind us how all earthly things are doomed to pass away;
That show the flowerets fading, and the fairest things depart,
And sometimes strike an aching chill of terror to the heart.
They tell us, in mysterious tones, that this is not our rest;
But we shall soon be happy 'mid the holy and the blest.

For when we leave the sunlight, that here always fades so soon,
We shall go into a cloudless land where it is always noon;
And when we leave the flowers that now so shortly fade away,
We'll live 'mid amaranthine flowers, for *there* is no decay;
For all that clothes in beauty's robe this changing land of earth
Is nothing to the glory in the world of heavenly birth.

For there the Saviour lives, and shows His everlasting love,
And joy, which heart imagines not, remains for us above :
No clouds of unbelief will hide the ever-smiling face,
As on our heads the crown of life His loving hand will place;
And perfect happiness and bliss will graciously be given,
For Jesus will be always there, and truly " Christ is heaven."

And so we would not always live in this dark world of pain;
But this shall be our prayer—that we may just so long remain
As 'twill take to fit us to belong to that immortal band,
Living in perfect holiness in that celestial land;
And when our mission is fulfilled, may some kind seraph come,
And bear us on His kindly wings to that oft-longed-for home.

The Tried and True.

"But thou, O Lord, art a shield for me; my glory, and the lifter up of mine head."—Psalm iii. 3.

DARKLY the clouds are gathering! The night
Draws on apace. The rough and noisy wind
Has blown upon the fragrant flowers that graced
The sunny landscape, and the fearful storm
Draws nearer and yet nearer. All around
Are boding voices; fearful whisperings
That speak of death and ruin. And athwart
The path I tread there are uprooted hopes,
And faded joys, and weeping memories!
O! but for one familiar voice to rouse
My drooping energies—to speak again
Kind words of cheer and courage!

                  Where are those
Who in the happy day gave loving smiles
And walked beside me? Where the gentle hand
That led me o'er the greensward? Gone! **all gone!**
And, in the moment of despair and woe,
I am alone! alone!

Yet stay, weak heart!
There is a light, a voice, a love!   Look up!
Ah, yes!   " Thy shield and glory !"

Other joys
Have passed in the chill night, but He has come
Nearer with each fresh sorrow, and my heart
Shall rest on Him until the darkness pass.

O, Father!   Friend above all other friends!
My head is lifted, for I trust in Thee!

Spare Useful Lives.

THE earth is groaning 'neath its weight of sin and agony;
Myriads of trampled, bleeding hearts in desolation lie;
Struggles and disappointments sharp around earth's toilers throng;
And youthful feet are halting 'twixt the paths of right and wrong.
Yet here and there, among the scenes of gloominess and night,
There are a few far nobler ones reflecting heaven's own light;
Bearing His lofty spirit who with guilt and sin yet strives;—
God of the vineyard, hear our cry—O, spare these useful lives.

Give power and vigour to the hand that opens but to bless:
Give brightness to the eye that beams with love and kindliness;
Strength to the ardent heart that throbs with constant sympathy,
And clearness to the brain that works for all around and Thee.
And for them all—O "lengthen out the brittle thread of life;"
And when their spirits faint, or grow half weary of its strife,
Then soothe the aching, burning brow, and on Thy sheltering breast
Give to the weak and fainting strength—give to the weary rest.

Yet spare, O spare them very long, in answer to our prayer;
Spare them to make this world of Thine more beautiful and fair;
Spare them to cheer the drooping soul, to whisper words of peace,
And urge the sorrowful to go where sorrows all will cease;
Spare them to labour still for Thee—these men of earnest heart—
And grant that in Thy blessing they may largely bear a part;
And O, that many souls unto their guidance may be given,
To meet and welcome them amid the ceaseless joys of heaven!

"Lord, Remember Me."

JESUS, from Thy throne above
   Bend Thine ear unto me now,
For my heart yearns for Thy love;
   Lay Thy hand upon my brow;
All my wishes turn to Thee;
Be my Friend—"remember me."

I am weary travelling here,
   Far from those I love the best:
And the pathway grows more drear;
   Thou alone canst give me rest:
Saviour, take me near to Thee;
'Mid heaven's light "remember me."

Friendship ever sweetens life,
   Fills joy's chalice to the brim,
Eases wretchedness and strife,
   Lights the sky when growing dim:
But no friends can equal Thee;
Holiest, "remember me."

In each bright and joyous hour,
　And in sorrow's deep distress—
For the griefs lose half their power
　That have Thee to aid and bless:
All in all I find in Thee;
Jesus, e'er " remember me."

My ungrateful, faithless heart
　Oft forgets the Friend I love;
Let me see Thee as Thou art;
　Call me to the worlds above.
Jesus then I'll ever be
Praising for remembering me.

"Thou, Lord, hast made me glad."

Psalm xcii. 4.

How great the beauty of the rock and river,
　The yellow corn-fields waving in their prime,
The wealth of leaves that in the breezes quiver,
　The golden sunset of rich autumn-time :
Their beauty brings deep gladness unto me;
I thank Thee, Lord, for they are all from Thee!

My days are ever some fresh pleasure bringing,
　And Providence has many smiles for me;
The opening clouds my Father's gifts are flinging—
　Gifts, like His love, unbounded, rich, and free;
And few, indeed, the circumstances sad:
I thank Thee, Lord, for Thou hast made me glad.

I know that Thou in love art always near me;
   I see Thy matchless impress everywhere;
In nature's choruses my heart can hear Thee;
   Thou art the Architect of all things fair;
And joy on earth would never gladden thus,
Were not Thy mercy ever over us.

Grant that my heart may cling not to Thy blessing
   So gratefully as it clings unto Thee;
And if Thy hand shall send me scenes distressing,
   I know that they will work for good to me.
O, while 'mid life's vicissitudes I stand,
Let me in ALL still recognize Thy hand!

The Untrodden Path.

GAILY the new year's greeting passed amid a joyous throng;
Stayed was the merry jest awhile, and hushed the flowing song:
Thoughts of the future came, but soon the laugh returned again;
Th' assembly was too joyous to admit a thought of pain:
And one more gay than all the rest smiled sweetly as she said,
"Happy! O, bright indeed will be the path my feet will tread.
The smiles and looks of gentle friends around me ever beam:
Life, while I've these to love me, must be happy as a dream."
She welcomed the untrodden path, but, ere twelve months rolled on,
The friends who made her happiness so very great were gone!

Another stood with trembling step on the threshold of the year;
His heart was sad with mournful grief, his spirit dark with fear;
The future had no beam of hope to light his lonely way—
The present was too desolate for one desire to stay.

And when they wished him happiness, he bitterly replied,
" Ere I had seen the opening year, O that I might have died!
Joy is for those who've home and friends—who are the loved and
    free,
The young, the beautiful, the good—*there is no joy for me.*"
But there was One All-loving Friend and Sympathizer near ;
He blessed the bleeding lonely heart, He sent a happy year.

Bright burns the fire, and round the hearth a little laughing band
Of happy, fair-haired children, with their tender mother, stand ;
Their faces are upturned to catch the ever-ready smile,
Unconscious how that mother's heart is thrilled with joy the while.
And when their prattling voices wish her many happy years,
Her eyes so eloquent with love have overflowed with tears.
" I know I shall be happy, for the treasures God has given
Have made my home a paradise, and earth almost like heaven."
The weeks roll by—those cheeks are pale—that bright eye now is
    dim—
God bless the little motherless—their parent is with Him !

O Father! the untrodden path how shall we dare to tread?
We see not what is in the clouds now hanging o'er our head.
Thou hid'st the future from our ken.   O ! be Thy children's light ;
Guide Thou our halting footsteps in the day or in the night.
Ourselves and our belovèd ones we do commend to Thee ;
Our refuge from the stormy blast, our Friend and Guardian be.
Give us whate'er Thou seest is best through all our future life ;
Shield from the noontide burning sun, the winter's storm and strife.
Each step we take, O Father, God, may we but feel Thee near,
And happier than earth could make will be the untried year.

Fading Away.

ALAS! the sweet flowerets are fading away,
The autumn winds blanch them with mournful decay;
A few weeks they lingered to gladden the earth,
In their loveliness seeming to smile on our mirth;
But the cold days are come, the beautiful things
Lie where the wind its sad cadences sings.

Sadness creeps over our reveries now,
Shadows autumnal now rest on *our* brow;
For we know that the flowers are not dying alone:
"Fading away" is the *heart's* mournful tone.
All we love best in this cold world of ours
Fadeth away like the beautiful flowers.

Leaving earth in its winter more barren and drear,
How quickly they pass to a happier sphere,
The friends that have smiled in our sweet summer-time,
And deepening the gloom that now darkens our clime!
O, it is sad that they too should decay,
And yet they are constantly fading away.

The pleasures that tended the days of life's spring,
That over its pathway such fragrance would fling,
How soon did they fade 'neath the chill breath of years!
They lived not in soil that was watered by tears,
But silently, rapidly, glided away,
Unheeding the voice that would urge them to stay.

And we, too, are fading—life's weakness comes on,
And youth's buoyant energies quickly are gone;

And eyes lose their brightness, the limbs lose their strength;
And the flashing thought ceases to dazzle at length ;
And the haughty step falters too oft on its way—
O yes! like the flowers, we are fading away.

Fading away—ever fading away!
'Tis well there's a country that knows no decay,
Where sweet amaranthines diffuse their perfume,
And aye wear the beauty of spring's youthful bloom.
O, for that wreath of unwithering flowers!
O, that that land in its beauty were ours!

Talk.

WHEN the fountain of gladness within thy heart
　　Is sending its waters high,
Wreathing the lip with its pleasant smiles,
　　And kindling the speaking eye;
When sorrow its icy hand has laid,
　　Depressing the buoyant heart,
Clouding the face with its look of pain,
　　Bringing affliction's dart—

Talk, for the blessings of sympathy
　　Will be in the answering tone,
And a deeper delight encircle thee
　　Than solitude e'er has known.
Let not thy heart be a sealèd book,
　　But reveal to the loving eye
That which inspireth the radiant smile,
　　Or causes the rising sigh.

Yes, talk—for a greater, more sacred gift
    Than language was never given;
But see that it copy, as best it may,
    Its spirit and tone from heaven.
See that its words are all words of love,
    That its meaning is kind and fair;
See that it rises in songs of praise,
    Or whispers the sound of prayer.

Suffering and Glory.

"For I reckon that the sufferings of this present time are not
worthy to be compared with the glory which shall be revealed in
us."—Rom. viii. 18.

"Not worthy," even when the fainting heart
    Lies crushed and bleeding 'neath the heaviest rod;
When called from every earthly joy to part,
    And tread the thorniest path man ever trod!

"Not worthy," though the whole short life were spent
    In prescient dread of evils yet to be;
Though light were never with our darkness blent,
    And the pent spirit never light and free!

"Not worthy," though for long and weary years
    Each step were o'er the grave of some dead joy,
And the long way we tread hedged in by fears,
    And cares and groans our sad and sole employ!

O, no! These sufferings of the present time
    Are nothing to the glory which remains
Within that sorrowless and sinless clime
    Where the calm heart is freed from all its pains.

That glory is too bright for human dream—
 So shadowless, so perfect, and so high—
When the bright "Morning Star," with fadeless beam,
 Shines ever sweetly on the kindling eye.

And those who suffered here shall there sit down
 By the still waters of the Saviour's love,
And cast at His dear feet the golden crown,
 And dwell *for ever* in that peace above.

O! let us take the sorrows for awhile,
 And in the darkest night still upward gaze
To that blest haven where our Father's smile
 Will lure us soon to swell the song of praise.

Why standest thou here idle?

Christian workman, art thou sleeping?
Hear'st thou not the wide world's weeping?
Hear'st thou not the wailing cry
That ascends to God on high ?

Rise, and make thy earth-home better ;
Strike the strong and iron fetter
From thy brother's aching hand—
From his brow the burning brand !

Canst not stay sin's vast undoing
Of the good thou art pursuing?
Hope and labour, strive and trust ;
They who pray to conquer, must !

Christian, surely thou wilt never
Live without a grand endeavour
To enhance thy country's fame—
Rise, and publish Jesus' name.

For the greatest greatness given
Is an heirship into heaven ;
Is an interest in the love
Of the Infinite above.

Rise and labour, then, my brother :
Let us, loving one another,
Lead the wanderer to God
Through the path the Master trod.

———

Jesus Only.

THE young man started early on his rough but upward way,
And sought memorials of those who passed from earth away ;
Said he, " My life shall copy all the greatest and the best
Who, in their pilgrimage sublime, earth's wilderness have pressed."
But ah ! they were not faultless ; he was soon obliged to own
That those who would be truly great must copy Christ alone.

Another sought to tread the paths that were most smooth and fair,
And studied every human chart with deep and patient care.
Alas ! he found that dangers lurked at every step he took,
Then turned for deeper lessons to the pages of the BOOK.
He saw that only those who in the Saviour's footsteps go
Walk where the living pastures are, and the still waters flow.

Another, pale and strengthless, lay upon the bed of death,
More languidly her eyelids drooped, more feebly came her breath ;
Those who had travelled with her through the flowery vales of life
Might go with her no farther through this path of awe and strife.
"Yet I am not alone," she said.   " The way grows chill and dim ;
But ' Jesus only' stays with me, and I am safe in Him."

Yes, blessed, holy Jesus! we shall go to all beside,
Until convinced our only home is at Thy bleeding side ;
More closely bind our hearts to Thee—loosen these human ties,
And ever to the Lamb of God turn our too-wandering eyes ;
Then take us to that world above where there are no more tears,
And " Jesus only" shall be praised through never-ending years.

Answers to the Saviour's Prayer.

"I pray not that thou shouldest take them out of the world, but that thou
shouldest keep them from the evil."—John xvii. 15.

THERE was a shroud of sadness on a pale and youthful brow,
A weight of crushing agony that caused her form to bow ;
That unfilled heart awoke at last to its deep sense of need,
And hungered for the love which human hearts so well can feed.
" O, for but one to love me !" was her wild, despairing cry ;
And one with smiling features and flattering lip drew nigh.
Nought in his mien proclaimed to her how he had laid the snare—
What stayed that yearning, youthful heart ?   It was the Saviour's
    prayer.

With arms crossed o'er his throbbing heart stood one in manhood's
    years—
'Twas terrible that eyes like his should shed such burning tears—
And all was fading from his life that he had lived to win ;
But one escaping way there seemed, and that the path of sin.

There was the tempter by his side still urging him to go,
And his weak spirit shrank from the alternative of woe ;
But, ah ! it passed—that bitter hour of trial and despair,
Nobly he triumphed, for for him was breathed the Saviour's prayer.

There was another—weak and frail; she had been used to cling,
All her long life, with tightened clasp, round some preserving thing;
And when the last was taken, there arose a bitter cry :
"I am too weak to stand alone ; O, if I could but die !"
And yet the fragile one fell not, for angel hands were spread,
And more than angel blessings came to the unsheltered head.
There was a heavenly power to clear the sin-polluted air ;
There was a shelter from the storm—there was the Saviour's prayer.

O ! there is evil constantly, above, beneath, around ;
Life is a cup in which excessive bitterness is found.
Its battle-sounds are ringing, and its danger presseth near,
Sin and temptation hover o'er, yet let not Christians fear.
There is a Friend who, 'mid it all, unstained, unscathed, has stood,
A Friend whose mighty, loving heart remembers us for good.
Let us walk softly through the path His friendship makes so fair;
Let us bless God if for our hearts arose the Saviour's prayer.

"Thy Way, O God, is in the Sanctuary."

Psalm lxxvii. 13.

BRIGHTLY the Sabbath morning dawned on the o'er-wearied earth,
A holy feeling reigned around, and hushed all boisterous mirth ;
Yet many mourned with aching hearts the roughness of the way,
As sighingly they gathered in the house of God to pray.

Sad looks there were on many brows, and up the sacred aisle
Few came with light and happy steps, few wore the heart-lit smile;
And yet some earnest, trusting ones before the altar trod,
To bathe within the streams that cheer the city of our God.

And sweetly, as 'twere music from the heavenly world, there stole
The Saviour's precious words of peace upon the weary soul;
The drooping spirit rose and clung more firmly unto Him,
And looked toward that better land which grief can never dim.

And faith grew stronger, deeper then, and hopes became more bright,
As the inheritance above half burst upon their sight;
And songs of praise from grateful hearts poured softly o'er the way :
Their thanks were for the house of God and for the Sabbath day.

O! when life's burdens on our hearts are pressing heavily,
God of the sanctuary, may we always look to Thee !
O, meet us in Thine own blest house, and light us as we go
With holy thoughts and brilliant hopes, to cheer the path below.

New Year's Day.

'Twas ushered in by prayer !   There knelt
   In many a consecrated room
Watchers and worshippers who felt
   How deep the silent midnight gloom!
And heavenward through the softened air
Rose solemn thoughts of secret prayer.

A few hours passed, and thousands trod
   Our English temples' well-worn aisles,
Listing the soothing words of God,
   And basking in the Saviour's smiles ;

Q

Gaining new comfort for the way,
From the sweet Sabbath new year's day.

And afterwards God's family
  Gathered around His table spread,
And Jesus 'mid them silently
  Blessed His disciples as they fed ;
And hearts were warmed by His deep love,
And eyes gazed longingly above.

The evening passed, but ere they slept
  What high resolves arose to heaven!
How many prayed, and loved, and wept!
  How many praised for sins forgiven!
Not loud, but deeply solemn words
Declared their lives henceforth the Lord's.

O, thanks that this important day
  Came on the *Sabbath* of our rest!
And as the year shall glide away,
  " God bless us, and we *shall* be blest!"
So sacredly did it begin,
May we ne'er darken it by sin!

Rise and Pray.

When thy home is far before thee,
And the dark clouds gather o'er thee ;
When the scenes are all distressing,
And the ills of life are pressing,
    Christian, rise and pray.

When thou'rt well-nigh broken-hearted,
When thy loved ones have departed,
When thou'rt very sad and lonely,
And art left with " Jesus only,"
   Mourner, rise and pray.

When, oppressed with pain and anguish,
Thou shalt lie, and shrink, and languish,
Dreading every fresh to-morrow,
Lest it bring increasing sorrow,
   Sufferer, rise and pray.

When the pleasant flowers are blooming,
All the joyous path perfuming,
And the sun is shining brightly,
And the hours are passing lightly,
   Gay one, rise and pray.

When thy life away is flying,
And in weakness thou art dying;
When the unseen is before thee,
And the swell of death is o'er thee,
   Lift thy heart, and pray.

Be not Discouraged.

BE not discouraged! In the darkest night
  Are hidden lamps,
Shedding above, around, the blessed light,
  Amid the damps.
Thou may'st not see the smiles that beckon thee!
But ever onward go, nor fearful be !

Be not discouraged!   For the true, brave heart
  Will seldom fail;
Who has the stern resolve to bear his part
  Will yet prevail.
If thou hast barriers to success, push on,
Till from thy smooth path they shall all be gone.

Be not discouraged!   Keep within thy breast
  Hope's brilliant beam:
Trust in thyself and God, and leave the rest,
  Nor idly dream;
But, looking ever on the sunny side,
Trust and go forward; for God will provide.

Be not discouraged, whatsoe'er thy lot;
  For God is near.
Still cheerily look up, and falter not,
  But persevere.
Be but courageous now, and all shall be
Blessed by thy Father, and made well for thee.

"They despised the Pleasant Land."

Psalm cvi. 24.

THERE is a land all beautiful
  Where fadeless flowerets bloom,
And sighs and sobs ne'er cleave the air,
  All laden with perfume;
But many turn despisingly,
  And choose a living tomb.

There are celestial music-strains,
  There living waters flow,
There the transported pilgrim band
  Unbroken rest may know.
Yet there are some would rather have
  The grief and toil below.

There constant pleasure dwells beneath
  The lofty, dazzling dome ;
And smiles of gladness wreathe the lips
  Of happy ones at home ;
Yet clinging to their misery
  Are some who rather roam !

O Father, may the pleasant land
  To us attractive be;
And may we love it more and more,
  Until its joys we see—
Till we are welcomed to our home,
  For ever safe with Thee !

" We all do fade as a Leaf."

Isaiah lxiv. 6.

WE all are fading ! Storms have beaten long
    Above, around ;
The wind sighs past us with its mournful song;
    The sodden ground
Clasps to its cold, damp bosom those who fall;
And, as the leaves drop, *we* are fading all !

We all are fading! Beautiful and bright
    Though some may bloom,
Beneath the verdure is the chilling blight;
    And to the tomb
Those who, so late, were joyous in the spring—
The loved, the lovely—all are gathering.

We all are fading! As the piercing blast
    Sweeps wildly by,
Perchance the summer of our life is past;
    And to the sky
The mournful requiem rises from the sod,
And we are dropping by the will of God.

We all are fading! But beyond the skies,
    Where seraphs sing,
Those of the Lord's transplanting shall arise
    T' eternal spring;
And, though all fading, may *we* gather where
God smiles, and all is beautiful and fair

I would not live alway.

I WOULD not live alway—though earth will entwine
Too closely its cords round this frail heart of mine
Though the joys and the friends that enrich it are dear,
And bountiful blessings are showered on me here,
My spirit oft yearns for a holier clime,
Where life and its pleasures are pure—are sublime.

I would not live alway—this is not my home,
Where sorrow and sin will so frequently come—
Where shadows may darken the sunniest day,
And dangers oft lurk in the loveliest way—
Where its scenes leave a void that no pleasure can fill,
And the thirsty soul tarries unsatisfied still.

I would not live alway—my fair fatherland
Allures me still on to its calm, peaceful strand;
The friends in its mansions are equally dear
With those that I love who are lingering here.
I long to dwell with them for ever in heaven,
Where the harp, and the crown, and the white robe are given.

I would not live alway—my Jesus is there,
Whom I long to behold 'mid the holy and fair;
I only half know Him, the glass is so dim
Through which my weak eyesight is peering at Him;
But, O! in that cloudless, that oft-longed-for place,
Enraptured I ever will gaze on His face!

I would not live alway—and yet while I stay
May I cheerfully toil through the difficult way—
Live and labour for Him whose ineffable love
Is training me now for the glory above!
So when death with its strife and its shadows comes on,
My Father may welcome His child with "Well done!"

For ever with the Lord.

Not for an hour or two,
Catching a distant view,
   Distant and dim ;
Not for a little space,
Gazing on Jesus' face—
   Ever with Him !

Not with a wandering heart,
Prone from His side to part,
   Weary and lone ;
Leaving His sheltering fold,
While my heart's love grows cold—
   Ever His own !

Not to displease Him so,
As every step I go,
   Slighting His love ;
But all my heart to give,
And in His smile to live,
   Ever above !

Not from the happy seat
At the Redeemer's feet
   Soon to be driven ;
Not to go back again
To the world's grief and pain—
   Ever in Heaven !

Ever to sweetly rest
On the Beloved's breast,
   Close to His side;
Near to Him still to be,
Through an eternity,
   There to abide!

Ever with Him I love,
Ever at home above,
   Happy and free.
Father! Thou hearest prayer;
Jesus! O, take me there,
   Ever with Thee!

By the Sea.

WHAT a motley group of faces
   Gather near the wondrous sea—
Calm and scornful, gay and laughing,
   Full of joy or misery!

See the young all smiles and gladness,
   And the old all full of care;
All the blithe and healthful happy,
   While the suffering breathe a prayer.

Ebbing, flowing, all unheeding,
   Rolls the deep and restless sea;
And the anthem of the waters
   Soundeth ever solemnly.

Now the pearly spray is breaking
   On the weedy, shell-strewn strand.
O ! the booming of the waters,
   Chorus infinite and grand !

And our hearts within are swelling;
   Tears unbidden dim the eye,
As we gaze upon the beauty
   Of the azure sea and sky.

As we list the glorious main,
   Filling all earth's lofty dome,
And the wind so wildly sweeping
   Over crested wave and foam.

O, Thou mighty One above us,
   Thou canst read the wordless thought :
Ever make all nature's grandeur
   With Thine own pure teachings fraught.

"The Earth, O Lord, is full of Thy Mercy."

Psalm cxix. 64.

High to Thy throne, O God, above the skies
The sins of feeble nations daily rise,
Thy pure commands Thy weakest creatures spurn,
   And from Thee turn.

And yet the flowers smile on, and day by day
The path is beautiful through which they stray;
Thy mercies slacken not, although they raise
   No song of praise !

Thou giv'st Thy children still their daily bread;
Through dark and dubious ways Thy hand has led;
Founts of Thy love gush by the steep hill-side,
　　With full, fresh tide!

Thou giv'st warm love, with precious household ties;
The sounds of mirth from happy hearths arise;
Yet they return the Giver of all Good
　　No gratitude!

O, Thou who weariest not—the Merciful—
Who mak'st all things so rich and beautiful—
When shall Thy children bring, on bended knee,
　　Heart-praise to Thee?

Recognition in Heaven.

Some think that on that brighter shore, toward which our worn feet
　　tend,
We shall not recognize the loved with whom we used to blend;
We shall not meet the speaking eye, nor clasp the fervent hand,
Of those whom we have loved so well within this colder land.
But, if earth's love were all we had to fill the spirit's need,
Alas for these fond hearts of ours! alas for love indeed!

But there's a voice within our souls, when these frail ties are riven,
That calms the throb of agony with precious words from heaven;
That checks the wild despairing cry, and leads the aching heart
To twine its tendrils round that home where we no more shall part.
O! *could* we call it *home* indeed if, though all else were fair,
We might not *love* amid its scenes, nor *know* each other there?

But *love must be immortal,* and its restless yearnings here
But the commencement of the joy within that perfect sphere.
Love is the atmosphere of heaven, and every ransomed one
Will be our friend and brother there, when conflict here is done.
But surely we shall love those best who, on our way to God,
Joined hands, and hearts, and interests, and blessed the path we trod.

Those who have passed away from us forget us not above;
They are not here to cheer us, but we have not lost their love.
A mother's lip, a sister's smile, will welcome when we go
As fondly as of yore, when they were toiling too below.
O, we shall *know* their greeting, and our pastors, teachers, there,
And love them, as we could not here, for all their kindly care.

Let us love on, then, evermore, and always cherish well
Thoughts of that happy meeting-place where we shall shortly dwell;
Where voices we have heard below will swell the blissful song;
Where parents, friends, and all we love, will join the white-robed
    throng;
Where, in unclouded happiness, we all shall lowly bend,
And worship Jesus perfectly—our best and dearest Friend.

"Thou knowest not what a Day may bring forth."

Prov. xxvii. 1.

"THOU knowest not!" The dense, dark cloud above
    Hideth its secrets close from mortal eye;
It may be full of deep and gentle love;
    It may bring justice from the fiery sky;
Deep mystery hangs o'er us every hour;
Uncertainty broods in the clouds that lower.

"A day may bring"—ah! what?   The hopes we reared
  May melt, like frost-work in the sun, away;
Or the deep grief may come not as we feared;
  Or disappointment's pain may pass away:
A single day may be with imports fraught
Too mighty even for our feeble thought.

The mighty man be stricken in his pride;
  The imprisoned soul be suddenly set free;
The loved, the loving, from our rent hearts glide
  On from our keeping, to eternity.
And darkness fall upon the narrow way;
And hearts be broken in a little day.

O Thou whose eyes can penetrate the gloom,
  We cling to Thee in all our helplessness.
Fit us for happy life, o'er the dark tomb:
  Be Thou with us in pleasure or distress.
The morrow, in its deep, deep mystery,
O Thou who doest well, we leave to Thee.

"Not this Man, but Barabbas."

John xviii. 40.

"Not this man."   Eager hands outstretch to grasp the failing hand,
To pluck the flowers that fade and droop upon the barren land,
To clasp to beating, hungry hearts the mocking, ashen food,
Yet fling with heedless folly far the highest, truest good.
"Not this man," though he bring with Him such high, immortal
    joys,
But fading pleasures, fleeting gifts, and worthless, foolish toys.

"Not this man." Some would vainly climb ambition's dazzling
  heights,
Nor heed the dense deep darkness that enshrouds the coming nights.
"Not this man." Some are choosing wealth to fill the hearts that
  yearn,
And from the Man of Sorrows in their scornfulness will turn.
"Not this man," "Pleasure's cup for me," the million wildly cries;
"Not this man, but Barabbas," still the shouts that reach the skies.

Ah! these are robbers all! They steal the peace, the purity,
God's stamp upon the noble brow—the manhood bold and free!
They take what nothing can restore, and leave bereaved and lone,
With aching head and bleeding heart, the bound despairing one.
There is no light, no joy, no hope for those who madly choose
The robber for their portion, and the Saviour-Friend refuse.

"Not this man!" He has love to give to every empty heart;
The sorrowful may cling to Him; He bears the sufferer's part;
And He will bless the eager soul with immortality,
Will fill the life with joyous wealth—will make it gain to die.
"Not this man!" Hast thou then no grief—no sin to be forgiven—
No thirsting after happiness—no longing after heaven?

"Not this man!" Stay awhile, and see —can any love so well?
Hast thou a shelter in the storm, a home in which to dwell,
Where sin and sorrow enter not? And can that heart of thine
Be satisfied with joy or love not holy or divine?
Jesus of Nazareth waiteth now thy answer to receive—
O, weary, heavy-laden one, cling unto Him and live.

Thanksgiving.

WE thank Thee, Father, who hast made us live,
   For the free current bounding through our veins,
For the wild ecstasy which life can give—
   The joy of being, even 'mid our pains;
We thank Thee for our reason's eager light,
The soul within us wonderful and bright.

We thank Thee for the beauties of the world,
   The mysteries of air, and sea, and sod,
Which Thou in Thy great goodness hast unfurled
   That we may see, and hear, and think of God,
And learn the unspoken lore of forest-trees,
And earnest whispers borne on passing breeze.

We thank Thee, Father, for the brotherhood—
   The warmth of tender heart and grasping hand,
The kindly nature seeking others' good—
   The free glad blessings of the household band,
The love that overflows from speaking eyes,
And thrills us with its eloquent replies.

We thank Thee for the discipline of life,
   . The hours of pain, and darkness, and despair;
The inner sorrow and the spirit strife
   That wrung from the sad heart a speechless prayer.
The trials have been blessings, and their spell
Has brought us nearer Thee who doest well!

We thank Thee, Father, for Thy deathless love,
   That follows us each onward step we take;
But most we bless Thee for the bliss above,
   When from the last long sleep we shall awake.
O Father, when these earth-cords shall be riven,
May our thanksgivings fill the courts of heaven!

Farewell.

FAREWELL, farewell! It has been feebly spoken
     By lips that paled;
And hearts have been bereaved and spirits broken,
     And hope has failed,
As suddenly upon the ear there fell
The withering blight of that dread word, Farewell!

Farewell, farewell! From loved ones that were dying
     Oft has it come,
And filled our hearts with mourning and with sighing,
     And in our home
Shrouded the day in darkness and despair—
Stolen the joy that smiled and blossomed there.

Farewell, farewell! It is not heard in heaven,
     Our home of rest!
There meetings, but no partings, will be given;
     All will be blest!
O that we all within that bourne may dwell,
Where lips ne'er falter, whispering Farewell!